Rising Wolf
The White Blackfoot

By

James Willard Schultz

Introduction

One of the greatest pleasures of my long life on the plains was my intimate friendship with Hugh Monroe, or Rising Wolf, whose tale of his first experiences upon the Saskatchewan-Missouri River plains is set forth in *Rising Wolf* just as I had it from him before the lodge fires of the long ago.

At first an *engagé* of the Hudson's Bay Company, then of the American Fur Company, and finally free trapper, Hugh Monroe saw more "new country" and had more adventures than most of the early men of the West. During the last years of his long life he lived much with his grandson, William Jackson, ex-Custer scout, who was my partner, and we loved to have him with us. Slender of figure, and not tall, blue-eyed and once brown-haired, he must have been in his time a man of fine appearance. Honest he was and truthful. Kind of heart and brave. A good Christian, too, and yet with no small[Pg x] faith in the gods of his Blackfoot people. And he was a man of tremendous vitality. Up to the very last he went about with his loved flintlock gun, trapping beavers and shooting an occasional deer.

He died in his ninety-eighth year, and we buried him in the Two Medicine Valley, under the shadow of the cliffs over which he had so many times helped the Pi-kun-i stampede herds of buffalo to their death, and in sight of that great, sky-piercing height of red rock on the north side of the Two Medicine Lake, which we named Rising Wolf Mountain. It is a fitting monument to the man who was the first of his race to see it, and the great expanse it overlooks.

J. W. S.

HUGH   MONROE'S   STORY
OF HIS FIRST YEAR ON THE PLAINS

CHAPTER   I
WITH THE HUDSON'S BAY COMPANY

You ask me for the story of my life. My friend, it would fill many volumes, for I have lived a long life of great adventure. But I am glad! You shall have the story. Let us set it forth in order. So! I begin:

I was born in Three Rivers Settlement, Province of Quebec, July 9, 1798. My father was Captain Hugh Monroe, of the English Army. My mother was Amélie de la Roche, daughter of a noble family of French *émigrés*. Her father owned a fine mansion in Montreal, and the large estate in Three Rivers, where my father lived with her what time he was not with his regiment on some expedition.

My childhood days were quiet enough. I played with the children of our peasantry; a Jesuit Father, resident with us, taught me a smattering of reading and writing in both French and English; and presently I got a gun, a beautiful, light smoothbore carrying thirty balls to the pound. From that time on it was always the gun with me. I ceased playing with the peasant children, and spent the most of my time hunting in the great forest surrounding the settlement. In my twelfth summer I killed my first deer. I shot two black bears when I was thirteen, and oh, how proud I was of that! An old pensioner of my mother's, a half-breed Montagnais Indian, too old and feeble to do much himself, taught me to trap the beaver, the otter, and the land fur-bearers, the fox, fisher, marten, and mink, and I caught many of them. Every spring my Grandfather de la Roche sold the pelts for me in Montreal for a good price, one winter catch, I remember, bringing me in[Pg 5] thirty pounds, which was a large sum for a boy to earn in a few months' time.

After the beginning of 1812 I saw little of my father, for then, you know, began the war between the English and the Americans, and he was with his regiment here and there, and took part in several battles. It was in the autumn of that year that my grandfather sent for us to move in to Montreal and live with him.

I did not like the town. I could neither hunt nor trap. I had little to do with the town boys; I did not understand their ways, so different from my ways. Mornings I attended the parish school; afternoons I rowed on the river, or visited in the warehouses of the Hudson's Bay Company, with which my grandfather had much to do. There I met *voyageurs* and trappers from far places—men dressed all in buckskin clothes, with strangely fashioned fur caps on their heads, and beaded moccasins encasing their feet. Some were[Pg 6] French, and some English, the one race having little to do with the other, but that made no difference with me; I made friends with both factions, and passed many, many pleasant hours listening to their tales of wild adventure, of fights with Indians, encounters with fierce bears of the Far West, and of perilous canoe trips on madly running rivers.

"That is the kind of life I want to lead," I said to myself, and, young as I was, began to importune my mother to allow me to engage with the great company. At first she but laughed at me. But as winter and summer and winter went by, and I never ceased my entreaties, not only to her, but to my grandfather, and to my father when he visited us, it became a matter not to be dismissed with idle jests.

And at last I had my way. "He was born for the adventurous life, and nothing else," said my father, "so we may as well let him begin now, and grow up to a responsible posi[Pg 7]tion with the company. Who knows but he may some day become its governor!"

It was my mother who objected to my going. Many a tear she shed over the little traveling-kit she prepared for me, and made me promise again and again that I would return to her, for a visit at least, at the expiration of my apprenticeship to the company. It was a fine kit that she got together for me, changes of underclothes, many pairs of stockings, several pairs of boots, an awl, and needles and thread, a comb and brush, and a razor, strop, and brush and soap. "You will need the razor later on. Oh, just think! My boy will be a bearded man when he returns to me!"

"Not if I can keep the razor. I despise whiskers! Mustaches! They are unclean! I shall keep my face smooth," I told her, and I have done so to this day.

When the time came for my going my father gave me a brace of silver-mounted pistols in holsters for the belt, and plenty of balls and[Pg 8] extra flints for them. My grandfather gave me twenty pounds, and a sun-glass. "There are times when flint and steel are useless, but as long as the sun shines you can always make fire with this," he told me. Little did we think what an important part it was to play in my first adventure upon the plains.

At last the day for my departure came. We had breakfast by candlelight and then my grandfather took us and my kit down to the wharf in his carriage. I went into the office and signed articles of apprenticeship to the Hudson's Bay Company for five years, at twenty pounds per year, and found, my father and mother signing as witnesses. Whereupon the chief clerk gave me a letter to the factor to whom I was to report without undue delay, Factor James Hardesty, at Mountain Fort, Saskatchewan River, foot of the Rocky Mountains, the company's new fort built for the purpose of trade with the little-known tribes of the Blackfeet, said to be a very numerous people, and possessors of a vast hunting-ground teeming with beaver and other fur animals.

My mother almost fainted when she learned how very far away was my destination. She wept over me, kissed me many times, and made me promise again and again that I would return to her at the end of the five years. And so we went from the office to the end of the wharf, where were the five big keel boats of the company, all loaded, and manned by the sturdy French and English *voyageurs*, and I got into one of them with my kit, smoothbore in hand and pistols at my belt, and the men cast off and bent to their oars. As far as I could see them, my father and mother and grandfather kept waving their handkerchiefs to me, and I waved mine to them. I never saw them after that day! It was May 3, 1814, about two months short of my sixteenth birthday.

As I have said, there were five boats in the flotilla, and each one was loaded with four or five tons of goods for the Indian trade, everything being done up in waterproof packages of about one hundred pounds weight. The heavy goods were mostly guns, powder and ball and flints, tobacco, beads, beaver traps, and brass and copper wire for making bracelets, and ear and finger rings, and axes, and copper and brass kettles of various size, and small hand mirrors. The lighter goods comprised blankets, red, blue, and yellow woolen cloth, needles, awls, thread, and the many other articles and trinkets sure to take the Red Man's fancy. Not a very valuable cargo, you may say, nor was it there in Montreal. But at Mountain Fort, foot of the Rocky Mountains, it would be of enormous value. There a gun was worth sixty beaver pelts—sixty pounds' worth of fur—and all the other articles sold in the same proportion. Why, a yard of tobacco—it was in long twists like rope—sold there for two beaver skins!

I shall say little of our long journey to Mountain Fort. It was interesting, but as nothing compared to what I saw and experienced after arriving at my destination. We turned into the Ottawa River from the St. Lawrence. How strange it seemed to me, a boy, to sit in the prow as strong men drove us fast and faster toward that unknown land.

We ascended the Ottawa as far as it was navigable, and then portaged our boats and cargoes from lake to lake across a divide, and finally, early in September, arrived at York Factory, on the Saskatchewan River, and close to where the stream empties into Hudson Bay. There we wintered, and set forth again as soon as the ice went out in the spring. *En route* I saw, for the first time, buffaloes, elk, and one or two grizzly bears, monstrously big bears they appeared to be, even at a distance. I also saw some camps of Cree Indians, enemies of the Blackfeet, but friendly to the whites, and was told that they feared to visit the fort to trade when the Blackfeet were there.

At last, after many weary days of rowing and cordelling up the swift Saskatchewan, we arrived at Mountain Fort. It was the 10th day of July, 1815. I had been a year and a couple of months on my way to it from Montreal!

The fort, built of logs, the buildings roofed with poles and earth, was in a heavily timbered bottom above the high-water mark of the river. It was enclosed with a high, log stockade, and had a bastion at one corner, in which were two small cannon. It was later to be known as Bow Fort, as the stream it was upon, which was a main tributary of the Saskatchewan, was called by the Blackfeet Bow River.

The fort bottom came suddenly into view as our boats rounded a sharp bend of the river, and my eyes and mouth opened wide, I guess, when I saw that its shore was crowded with Indians, actually thousands of them. They had seen few white men, and few boats other than the round "bull boats" which they hastily constructed when they wanted to cross a river, and our arrival was of intense interest to them.

I noted at once that they were far different from all other Indians that I had seen on my long trip across the country. They were much taller, lighter of skin, and slenderly and gracefully built. I marveled at the length of hair of some of the men; in some instances the heavy braids touched the ground; five feet and more of hair! A very few of them wore blankets; the rest were dressed in well-tanned leather—call it buckskin if you will—garments, sewed with sinew thread. But these were well made, and very picturesque, ornamented, as many of them were, with vivid embroidery of porcupine quills, dyed all the colors of the rainbow. Men, women, and children, they all, excepting the few possessors of our com pany blankets, wore wraps, or togas, of buffalo cow leather, those of some of the men covered with bright-painted pictographs of their adventures, and strange animals of their dreams. I noticed that few of the men had guns; the most of them carried bows and arrows in fur or leather cases and quivers at their backs.

As we swept past the great crowd of people toward the landing, my heart went out to every one of them. I wanted to know them, these people of the plains, as yet unaffected and unspoiled by intercourse with the whites. Little did I think how very soon I was to know them, and know them intimately!

At the landing the factor, Hardesty, and some of his employees, backed by a half-circle of chiefs, awaited our coming. Little attention was paid to me, just a boy. The factor greeted the head *voyageur* of our flotilla, then the men, and then seemed suddenly to discover me: "And you—" he stopped and stared at me, and said impatiently to one whom I afterward learned was his clerk: "I asked for men, and they send me a boy!"

Then he turned again to me and asked: "Well, young man, what brings you here to this wild land?"

"I came to work, sir!" I answered, and handed him the letter which the company clerk had given me in Montreal. He read it and his manner toward me instantly changed.

"Ah, ha! So you are Hugh Monroe, Junior!" he exclaimed. "And you have come out to grow up with the company! I know your father well, young sir. And your Grandfather de la Roche as well. Fine gentlemen they are. Well! Well! We shall find some use for you, I am sure." And he shook hands with me, and then, after a time, told me to accompany him to his quarters.

We went up the broad beaten path in the timber to the fort, and the big, hewn timber gate swung open for us, and its keeper bowed low as he let us in. "We keep a guard here night and day, and two men up there with the cannon. We have many Indians hereabout, and as yet do not know them well," the factor told me.

We went into his quarters, a big room with an enormous fireplace at one end. It had windows of thin, oiled rawhide, which let in a yellowish light. Its furniture was home-made and comprised a desk, several chairs, a bunk, piled high with buffalo robes and blankets, and an elkhorn rack supporting several guns. I was told to put my gun and pistols on the rack, that another bunk should be put up, and that this was to be my home for the present.

We soon went out, for a long line of employees was bringing in the cargoes from the boats, and the factor had to inspect them. I made my way to the upper floor of the bastion and entered into conversation with the two men on guard there with the cannon, and looked down now and then at the great crowd of Indians out in front of the stockade. Many of them had bundles of beaver and other fur which they were waiting to trade for the newly arrived goods. The watch told me that they had been encamped at the fort for two months awaiting the coming of the boats, and that they had more fur than the cargoes of the five boats could buy, unless the factor more than doubled the price of the goods. That didn't seem possible to me.

"Why, how many Indians do you think are here?" asked one of the watch.

"Three or four thousand?" I hazarded.

He laughed. "Make it thirty thousand, and you will come nearer hitting it," he told me, and I gasped.

"There are a lot more than that," said the other watch, confidently.

"Yes, I guess there are," the first went on. "You see, young fellow, we have here right now all three tribes of the Blackfeet, and their allies, the Gros Ventres, and Sak-sis. Yes, there's probably between thirty and forty thousand of them, all told."

Again I gasped.

"Why, if they wanted to, they could take this fort without any trouble!" I exclaimed.

"Take it! Huh! In just two minutes all would be over with us if they started in. These are the boys that keep them from doing it," he said, and patted the cannon beside him.

"You see that cottonwood tree out there, how its limbs are all splintered and dead?" said the other watch. "Well, we fired a four-pound charge of trade balls into it just to show them what it would do. There was a big crowd out there before the gate, as big as there is now, and when we touched her off you should have heard the women and children yell, and seen 'em run for cover. The men, most of them, jumped when the old gun boomed, but they stood their ground and stared and stared at the shower of leaves and twigs coming down. We then fired the other one, and down came about all of the rest of the tree-top. I bet you they said to one another: 'It's no use trying to take that fort; those big guns would cut us all down just as they did the tree-top!'"

"But we are taking no chances," said the other. "You see that little gate in the big gate? Well, when the Indians come to trade we let them in through it, a few at a time, making them leave their weapons outside, and just as long as the trade lasts we keep one of the cannon pointed to the door of the trade-room."

"And do you never leave the fort and the protection of the guns?" I asked, thinking how hard it would be for me to remain shut up in the fort, never to visit in the camps of the Indians, or hunt the game with which the country teemed.

"Oh, we go out whenever we want to," said one. "You see, they wouldn't pot just a few of us, for fear that they couldn't trade here any more, and they are crazy for our goods. No, unless they can kill us all and take the fort at one swoop, we shall never be harmed by them, and it is only at a time like this, when the trade-room is full of goods, that there is any danger. Anyhow, that is the way I look at it."

"And right you are," the other watch agreed.

Just then the factor called to me that it was dinner-time, and I left the bastion and followed him into a room where the cook, a French-Huron woman, wife of one of the employees, served us our simple meal. It consisted solely of buffalo meat and strong black tea, and the factor explained that he, as well as the employees, lived upon meat and the various fruits of the country, fresh and dried, the year around. Christmas was the one exception; on that day every one had a generous portion of plum pudding with his meat dinner! You can see how it was in those days. Freight was a year *en route* to that far place from Montreal, and every pound of it had to be merchandise for the Indian trade. At a rough guess I should say that every pound laid down at the fort was worth from three to twenty guineas per pound in fur. Copper wire made into bracelets and other jewelry, for instance, was worth a hundred guineas, a hundred beaver skins, per pound. Naturally, the orders from London were that factors and employees alike must be satisfied with the one big treat, plum pudding for the Christmas dinner! Well, it didn't matter. We became so accustomed to a meat diet that we gave little thought to other food. In summer, when in turn the service berries, choke-cherries, and bull berries ripened, we feasted upon them, and the women dried some for winter use, not enough, however, for more than an occasional dish, stewed, and without sugar, rather flavorless.

We finished our meal and some of the employees took our place at the table after we went out. Factors of the company did not eat with the men. In fact they did not associate with them. They held themselves aloof, and ruled their forts with stern justice. They generally issued their orders through their clerks.

After the men had finished their dinner, the great occasion of the year, the trade, was opened by a feast to the chiefs of the different tribes. They came into the fort followed by their women, staggering under loads of fur, and the factor sat with them while they ate, and smoked with them afterward. After the pipe had gone the rounds, the chiefs one by one made speeches, very badly interpreted by a man named Antoine Bissette, a French-Iroquois half-breed who had married a Cree woman who had some knowledge of the Blackfoot language, and through her had acquired a few words of it. Each chief made a long speech, and at the end of it the interpreter would say: "He says dat he is friend to whites. He say dat you his brudder. He say dat he give you hees pack of furs what hees woman she has dere!"

"And what else did he say?" the factor would ask.

"An' dat is all."

"And that is all! Huh!" the factor exclaimed. "Here we have had long speeches, matters of importance to the trade may have been touched upon, and you can't tell me what has been said! I told you a year ago, Antoine, to study this language, but you do not improve in it. If anything, your interpreting is worse than it was last spring!"

"But what can I do? My woman, he is mad all the time. He say Blackfoot language no good; no will talk it. So, me, I no can learn."

"Huh!" the factor again sputtered, and with a shrug of the shoulders and a wave of the hand, led the way to the trade-room. There he gave the chiefs good value for their furs, and presents besides, and they retired, well satisfied, to make room for their people.

I spent all of the afternoon in the trade-room watching them, and saw much to interest and amuse me. The men, almost without exception, bought guns and ammunition, traps, and tobacco, and the women bought the finery. I saw one young woman pay twenty beavers for a white blanket, and proudly drape it around the stalwart form of her man. He wore it for a few minutes, and then put it over her shoulders, and when his turn came to trade he bought for her several skins' worth of copper jewelry. I saw many such instances during the trade of the next few days, and one idea of the Indians that I had—that the men took everything and merely tolerated their women, used them as mere slaves—went glimmering.

The next morning the factor told me that he would give me the day off, and advised that I spend it in visiting the camps of the different tribes, located in the river bottoms above the post. He assured me that I should be perfectly safe in doing so, and said that I had best leave my gun at home, so as to show the Indians that we regarded them as the friends that they professed to be. I did, however, thrust one of my pistols under my shirt-bosom and, upon Antoine's advice, wore a blanket Indian fashion, so the camp dogs would not bother me.

Thus equipped, I set forth.

I had a wonderful day, a day of a thousand surprises and intense interest. The trail to the next bottom above the fort ran over a point of the plain ending in a bank at the river, and looking out from it I saw that the plain for several miles was covered with the horses of the different tribes, actually thousands and thousands of them, all in bands of from sixty or seventy to two or three hundred head. I afterward found that each owner so herded his horses that they became attached to one another, and would not mix with other herds.

From the point I looked down upon the camp in the next bottom, the camp of the Pi-kun-i, or so-called Piegans, the largest tribe of the Blackfoot Nation, and tried to count the lodges. I actually counted fourteen hundred and thirty, and afterwards estimated that there were four hundred more pitched in the timber bordering the river. Well, say that there were eighteen hundred lodges, and five persons to the lodge; that made a tribe of nine thousand people!

I went down into the camp, keeping an eye upon the great wolf-like dogs lying around each lodge. Children were playing everywhere around, and the river was full of them, swimming. Women were busy with their daily tasks, cooking meat, tanning leather, or removing the hair from hides with oddly shaped elkhorn hoes tipped with steel or flint, or else sitting in the shade of the lodges gossiping, and sewing garments with awl and sinew thread, or embroidering them with colored porcupine quills. Men were also gathered in little groups, chatting and passing great stone-bowled, long-stemmed pipes from hand to hand. It was all a peaceful and interesting scene.

I did not go through the whole camp; I somehow felt bashful before so many people; but as far as I went all smiled at me pleasantly as I passed, and spoke to me in kindly tones. How I wished that I could know what they said! How I wanted to know the meaning of the strange symbols with which some of the lodges were painted! On some were paintings of animals; buffalo, otter, beaver, deer, all with a red line running from the mouth back to a triangular figure in red in the center of the body. No two lodges, with one exception, were painted alike. On many of them, perhaps most, was painted, close up to the smoke-hole and at the rear, a symbol shaped much like a Maltese cross. I determined to ask Antoine what all the paintings signified.

From this camp I went on up the river to the others, those of the Sik-si-kah, or Blackfeet proper, and the Kai-na, or Bloods; these two and the Pi-kun-i comprising the three tribes of the Blackfoot Nation. And beyond them I looked down from the edge of the plain at the big camp of the Ut-se-na, or Gros Ventres, and last, that of the Sak-sis, or Heavy Talkers, a small Athabaskan tribe which had long been under the protection of the Blackfeet, as I learned later.

That evening I asked Antoine many questions about what I had seen, only to find that he could not answer them. Nor could any of the employees. Through the open doorway between the cook-room and his quarters the factor heard my futile questioning and called to me. I went in. He had me close the door, and then asked me a question that made me gasp.

CHAPTER II

THE SUN-GLASS

"How would you like to travel about with the Pi-kun-i for a time, and learn their language?"

I could only stare at him, hardly believing my ears, and he added: "I am sure that you would be in no more danger than you are here in the fort, or I would not propose this."

"I would rather do it than anything else! It is just what I want to do!" I told him.

"Let me explain the situation to you fully," he went on. "But, first, did you ever hear of Lewis and Clark?

"No? Well, they are two American Army officers who, a few years ago, led an expedition from the Mississippi River up the Missouri River to its head in the Rocky Mountains, and thence down the waters of the Oregon to its confluence with the Pacific Ocean. They were the first white men ever to see the country at the headwaters of the Missouri, and between it and the ocean. Now, in the dispatches that came to me with the goods, yesterday, I received most disturbing news: Following the trail of Lewis and Clark, our rival, the American Fur Company, is pushing westward and establishing posts on the Missouri, the upper part of which is in our own territory. I am ordered to learn if it has entered our territory, and if so, to take steps to block its trade with our Blackfoot tribes. The Pi-kun-i are going south to the Missouri plains for the summer as soon as they finish their trade with us, and I want you to go with them, and, while learning their language, keep an eye out for our rivals. I can't trust Antoine to do this, and anyhow he will never become a good interpreter. I believe that you will soon master the language."

Of course the factor was mistaken. The Missouri River country was not in our territory. We were to learn that later. Nor did we then have any idea of the vast extent of the hunting-ground of the Blackfeet. It was for me to discover that it extended from the Saskatchewan, yes, even from the Slave Lakes, south to their Elk River of the South, which is the Yellowstone River of the whites, and from the Rocky Mountains eastward for an average width of more than three hundred miles. A part of it, from the tributaries of the Missouri south, had been Crow country, but the Blackfeet had driven them from it. The Pi-kun-i, with their allies, the Ut-se-na, or Gros Ventres, lived for the greater part of the time in the southern part of it, along the Missouri and its northern and southern tributaries, and the other two tribes, with their Athabaskans, the Sak-sis, liked best the plains of the Saskatchewan and its tributaries.

Before the advent of the horse the Blackfeet tribes had all lived in the Slave Lake country. The Crees had so named these great bodies of water, for the reason that in that far-away time the Blackfeet made slaves of the enemies they captured. As nearly as I could learn, it was between 1680 and 1700 when the Blackfeet began to obtain horses by raids far to the south, even to Old Mexico, and in 1741 or 1742 obtained a few guns from the post on the Assiniboine River founded by the Sieur de la Vérendrie, that unfortunate explorer who was the first white man to see the Rocky, or as he named them, the Shining, Mountains. With both guns and horses, the Blackfeet were not long in taking possession of the rich game country to the south of the Slave Lakes, and driving from it not only the Crows, but other tribes as well.

On the day after my talk with the factor, he had an interview with Lone Walker, head chief of the Pi-kun-i, to which I was an interested listener. It was agreed, as well as Antoine could explain the matter, that I was to travel south in his care, living in his lodge, and riding his horses, and that upon bringing me safe back to the fort when he and his tribes returned to trade, he should be given a gun, two blankets, and two lengths of twist tobacco. Rich presents, indeed! More than enough, as the factor said, to insure his taking the greatest care of me. And anyhow my heart went out to the chief. Tall, dignified in bearing, his handsome face and eyes expressive of a kind and honest nature, I felt from the start that he would be a good friend to me, and I was not mistaken. I little realized at that time, however, what a really great man he was with his people.

Owing to their desire to start south at once, the Pi-kun-i were the first to trade in their take of furs. They were a matter of ten or twelve days doing it, and in the meantime I kept pretty close in the trade-room listening to Antoine's interpretations of their needs, and memorizing the words. In that way I learned their names for the different trade articles, and a few helpful sentences as well, such as the equivalent in their language for "What is it?" "Where is it?" "What is it named?" and so on. And then, one day, I saw Antoine's wife sitting with a Sak-si woman, the two apparently conversing with one another by means of signs. I asked Antoine about it and learned that it was the sign language, used by all the tribes of the plains; that almost anything could be told by it, even stories, and that his wife understood it very well.

"Then why don't you learn it? Would it not be of great help in your interpreting?" the factor asked him.

"I am try! I am do my possible! Sare, honneur, my han's, my fingare, he is not queek to do it!" he answered.

"Huh! Antoine, you're a fool! Yes, and so am I, or I would have known about this sign language, and have learned it long since!" the factor exclaimed.

"My woman, she will teach it to you; I will help," Antoine volunteered.

We began lessons with her that very evening, and before I left I had pretty well learned it. The signs are invariably so significant of the thought to be expressed, that, once seen and understood, they are not easily forgotten. I know not where the sign language originated, but I think that it came to the people of the plains from Mexico, spreading from one tribe to another until it finally reached the Blackfeet. The tribes of the forests, and of the two coasts, and the Great Lakes, knew it not.

At last the morning came upon which the Pi-kun-i were to break camp. On the evening before Lone Walker had sent my outfit of things over to his lodge, ready to be put upon one of his pack horses, and now, leading a horse for me, he came to the fort with his under-chiefs for a farewell meal and smoke with the factor.

I hastily ate my morning meat and, while the smoking was going on, saddled and bridled the horse. The factor had given me his own light, English, hunting-saddle, and I thought it a very comfortable one to ride upon. Later, when I got from a warrior a Spanish saddle that he had taken in a raid far to the south, I learned what comfort in riding really was!

The horse saddled, I said good-bye to the men. The *voyageurs* with whom I had come to the fort were soon to load the boats with furs and return to York Factory, and eventually Montreal, and I handed the head man a letter for my mother, telling her of my safe arrival at the fort, of the thousands of wild Indians that I had seen, and the expedition upon which I was about to embark. If all went well, she would receive it in about a year's time.

The round of smoking ended, the chiefs came out with the factor, and I said a last good-bye to him, and we mounted and set forth.

There were just twenty-four of the chiefs, one for each band, or gens, of the Pi-kun-i—Lone Walker, as I afterward learned, being chief of the I-nuk-siks, or Small Robes Band, as well as head chief of the tribe. With them were five other men, each wearing his hair done into a huge, fur bound knot on the foretop of his head, the insignia of the sun priest, or so-called medicine man. None of the party wore war bonnets, or war costumes, and that rather surprised me. I soon learned that they were never worn except when the men were going into battle—if there was time to put them on, and when dancing, or observing some great religious ceremony. No! The decked-out Indian, hunting, or traveling, or sitting about in camp, and the Indian wearing nothing but a breech clout and a pair of moccasins, is just the Indian of the artists' dreams! My Indians wore plain leather shirts, and wide-flapped leggings, and quill-embroidered moccasins, and their wraps were also of leather, some of them painted with pictographs of the wearer's adventures in war and hunting.

But for all that they were picturesque enough. Each one carried a shield slung from the left arm, and bow and arrows in a case and quiver at the back, and a gun across the saddle front. Beautifully dyed quill embroidery on the fringed leather pipe and tobacco sacks dangling from their belts, and the bright, painted symbols on the covering of their shields gave the needed color to their otherwise somewhat soberly plain, everyday wear.

And what splendidly built men they were! What fine features they had, and the small, perfectly formed hands and feet of real gentlemen. And I learned that they had the manners of gentlemen. That in their daily intercourse they were ever courteous to one another. That their jesting and joking was never rude or coarse, and how they did love a good joke and laugh! And proud they were, of their lineage, and their war records, and their women and children, of their great herds of horses, and their vast domain. But it was a just and natural pride, in no way different from the pride of our own best people. And with it was great kindliness of heart and ready proffers of help for all the unfortunate, for widows and orphans, the old and the sick. Such were the old-time Blackfoot chiefs.

Camp had been broken while the chiefs were saying their farewells in the fort, and now, as we rode out upon the plain from the river bottom, we saw the great caravan strung out away ahead of us and to our right. It was like a huge snake making its way southward over the ridges and the hollows of the plain, a snake about three miles in length!

It was advancing at a slow trot, and at a livelier pace we rode along its length to take the lead. Each family had its place in it, the women and children riding pack and travois horses, the men and youths driving the loose ones. The trappings of the horses, broad leather breast bands and cruppers, blazed with color, beautifully worked designs of porcupine-quill embroidery. The quaintly shaped *parflèches*, fringed pouches and sacks of rawhide and leather, upon the pack horses were brightly painted. Some horses, generally white ones daubed with red ochre, the sacred color, carried nothing but the pipe and pouches of a medicine man, and were always led. The lodge-pole horses dragged, generally, four lodge poles, two fastened to each side of the saddle by the small ends, and these and the ends of the travois poles scraped harshly into the plain and wore deeper than ever the many furrows of the broad trail.

As I rode with the chiefs along the edge of the long column I believe that every man, woman, and child of it gave me a smile, and some sort of greeting —one of which, "Ok-yi, nap-i-an-i-kap-i!" (Welcome, white youth), I already knew. And to all I replied: "Ok-yi, ni-tuk-a!" (Welcome, friend), which was a sad error when addressed to a woman or girl, embarrassing them, and causing all who heard to laugh. But the greetings and the smiles gave me heart; I felt that I was already liked by these people of the plains, and that was pleasant. I certainly liked them.

We passed the long column and rode on ahead of it, but not in the real lead. Ahead of us several hundred men, the scouts for the day, rode spread out like a great fan far to the right and left of the trail, as well as some of them upon it. They were not hunting; time and again we saw herds of buffaloes and antelopes rushing off out of their way, and none pursued them.

It was about noon when, topping a low ridge, Lone Walker led us a little to one side of the trail and dismounted. So did we all, tethering our horses to bunches of sage or greasewood, and then sitting in a little circle on the top of the rise. A medicine man unfastened the fringed and embroidered sack dangling at his belt and, getting out pipe and tobacco and some dried leaves of *l'herb* to mix with the tobacco, made leisurely but careful preparations for a smoke. First he thoroughly cleaned the huge, black, stone bowl, blowing through it, and then the separate, long, carved wooden stem, to make sure that they were clear. Then he fitted them together, and little by little filled the bowl with the mixture of tobacco and *l'herb*, tamping down each pinch with a small, blunt-ended stick. This done to his entire satisfaction, he unslung from his shoulder a section from a birch tree, about four inches in diameter and six inches in length, removed its wooden stopper, and I saw that it was hollowed out, and clay lined. Turning the mouth of the strange receptacle to the ground, he gave it a rap or two and out came a piece of partly charred punk wood which he quickly picked up and blew upon, and I realized that this was the Blackfoot way of keeping fire. But, blow as he would, there came no glow in the punk, no rise of smoke. The fire was out.

With an exclamation of disappointment the man dropped the punk back into place, put in the stopper, meantime looking around the circle to see if any one carried one of these fire boxes, as I may call them. None did. Here and there a man spoke, evidently remarking upon his disappointment. And then, suddenly, I thought of my grandfather's present to me, the sun-glass in the pouch at my side, and I called out to the medicine man: "I will light it for you!" In my excitement I forgot that he knew no word of my language.

But I had called his attention to me, and that of all the others too. They watched me closely as I fumbled in the pouch for the glass, drew it out and removed its silk wrapping. Having done that, I made signs to the medicine man to put the stem of the pipe to his mouth. He did so, and I focused the glass upon the charge of the tobacco mixture in the bowl. Almost at once it began to turn black and a thin streak of smoke to rise from it, and, drawing steadily upon the stem, the medicine man filled his mouth with smoke, his eyes growing bigger and bigger, until at last he let out a great blow of it, and then, with a shout of surprise, sprang to his feet and held the pipe aloft toward the sun. At that all the other chiefs sprang up, and shouting I knew not what, made a rush for me, and I believed my time had come!

Antoine had told me that the Blackfeet—as he called them, the heathen Blackfeet—worshiped the sun. The thought flashed through my mind that I was to be killed for using the sacred fire of their god! And as wild-eyed, excited, shouting chiefs came crowding around me I threw up my hands, in one of them the fateful glass, and cried: "I did not mean harm! It is a glass, nothing but a glass!"

As though they could understand! Or my pitiful cry save me!

But suddenly, instead of blows I saw that Lone Walker and others nearest me were stroking my shoulders, my breast, and back with their open hands, and then their own bodies, and the others, crowding, reached in between them and touched me wherever they could, and then stroked themselves, meantime shouting something to the head of the passing caravan.

Out from it rushed all who heard, men and women, and sprang from their horses and surged in to me, women frantically edging in under the arms of the men and rubbing their suckling infants against any part of my body that they could reach. And still badly frightened, I thrust the glass into Lone Walker's hand and made signs the best I could that I gave it to him. With a shout he held it aloft, tears streaming from his eyes, and began what I sensed must be a prayer to the sun. At that a great hush came upon the ever-increasing crowd. All listened closely, occasionally crying out something that I afterward learned was as we would say: "Yes! Yes! Have pity upon us all, O sun!" Then, presently, he finished the prayer, and looking around at the people addressed a few words to them. Whereupon they mounted and resumed their places in the column, and moved on.

The chiefs, however, again sat down in a circle, Lone Walker signing to me to sit beside him, and the pipe was passed from hand to hand, each one in turn taking a few whiffs of smoke from it and blowing it first toward the sun, and then to the ground. At last the pipe came to me. I passed it on to the chief on my right, but he instantly handed it back and gave me to understand that I was to smoke. I did so, blowing the smoke to sky and earth as I had seen the others do, and then passed it on. I had never smoked. The taste of it was bitter and nauseating in my mouth; my head soon began to swim and I felt terribly sick for a long time. I did not smoke again until I was past my twenty-fifth birthday.

Well, when the pipe was smoked out and put away we mounted our horses and rode on, I still sick but quite over my scare. Word of what I had done, of my bringing down sun fire, had evidently passed back the entire length of the column, for as I rode on to the head of it with the chiefs the people all called out to me again, and this time with a new name for me, and in their manner respect, even awe, was evident enough. They called me now, "Nat-o-wap-an-i-kap-i," which I thought had to do with the sun (nat-os). I was right; I soon learned that the word meant sun youth, or sacred youth. I was very proud of the name, and very glad of my grandfather's happy thought in selecting the glass for me. True, I had brought it this long way across the plains only to part with it, but my one chance use of it had given me important standing with the tribe.

We traveled on steadily ahead of the column until about four o'clock in the afternoon, and then once more dismounted and gathered in a circle, this time on the edge of a long slope running down to the timbered valley of a small stream. Again the medicine man got out his pipe and filled it, and I taught Lone Walker how to light the charge with the sun-glass, every one intently watching, and making exclamations of wonder and satisfaction when the feat was accomplished. This time I firmly passed the pipe when it came to me, and while the chiefs smoked and chatted I watched the long procession of the tribe pass down the slope into the valley, and scatter out over a big, grassy flat on the far side of the creek. There the horses were relieved of their burdens, and a few minutes later every lodge of the camp was up in place, and the women were carrying into them their various family belongings, and going for wood and water. All that was the women's work; the men sat about until all was completed.

As soon as the pipe was smoked out we got upon our horses and rode slowly down the slope to the creek, and then scattered out into camp. Lone Walker led me to the southwest part of the big circle of lodges, which was the allotted place for his band, the Small Robes, and to one of two immense lodges, which were both his property.

We got down from our horses, and I was about to unsaddle mine, when a woman took him from me, and signed that I was to follow the chief into the lodge. I did so, and, making a step in through the doorway, heard a growling and snorting that made my heart jump. And well it might, for there on each side of me, reared back and hair all bristled up, was a half-grown grizzly bear!

I dared not move, neither to retreat, nor go forward, and thus I stood for what seemed to me hours of time, and then Lone Walker scolded the bears and they dropped down at rest and I passed them and went to the place pointed out to me, the comfortable couch on the left of the chief's.

I think that the chief allowed me to stand so long facing the bears, just to try me; to learn if I had any nerve. I was glad that I had not cried out or fled. I soon became friendly with those bears, and often played with them. It has been said that grizzlies cannot be tamed. Those two were tame. They had been captured when small cubs, so small that they made no resistance to being taken up, and for months had been held up to the teats of mares, there to get the milk without which they could not have lived. I may say here that they disappeared one night in the spring of their third year, and were never seen again. They had at last answered the call of their kind.

It was with intense interest that I looked about the lodge, the first that I had ever entered, and which was to be my home for I knew not how many months.

It was a lodge of twenty-eight buffalo cow skins, tanned into soft leather, trimmed to proper shape to fit together, and sewed with strong sinew thread. It was all of twenty-four feet in diameter, and the lodge poles were at least thirty-six feet long, and so heavy that a horse dragged but two of them. There were thirty poles, and the lodge skin was in two sections. All around the inside was a leather lining running from the ground up to a height of about six feet, and attached to a rawhide line running from pole to pole. This made an air space between the lodge skin and the lining of the thickness of the poles. The pegged lodge skin did not reach the ground by four inches or more, so the air rushed in under it, and up between it and the lining, and out of the top of the lodge. This created a good draught for the fire and carried off the smoke. No air came in through or under the lining, it reflected the heat of the fire, and because of this simple construction the lodge was warm and comfortable even in the coldest winter weather. The lining was brightly painted, the design being a series of three different long, narrow, geometric figures distinctively Blackfoot.

All around the lodge, excepting on each side of the doorway, were the couches of the occupants, ten in number, a slanting back-rest of willow slats at the head and foot of each one. In the triangular spaces thus left between the couches, and on each side of the doorway, were stored no end of *parflèches*, bags, pouches, and leather-wrapped bundles containing the property of the different occupants of the lodge. Besides Lone Walker and myself, there were eight women and nine children, ranging from babies up to boys and girls twelve and fourteen and eighteen years old, the latter being a boy named I-sas-to, or Red Crow, whose couch and sitting-place I was to share.

Be not shocked or surprised when I tell you that Lone Walker had nineteen wives. Eight were in this lodge. The others and their children, and the chief's old father and mother were in the adjoining, big, twenty-eight-skin lodge. At first this polygamy was very repugnant to me; but I soon saw how necessary it was. The Blackfeet men were continually falling in battle with their many enemies, and only by becoming plural wives could the large preponderance of women be cared for.

Lone Walker's first, or head wife, named Sis-tsi-ah-ki, or Little Bird Woman, was a fine-looking woman of about thirty-five years. She was one of the happiest persons I have known. There was always a smile on her face, she sang constantly at her work, and her heart was as good as her smile; she was always doing something nice for others. In a way she was the head, or supervisor of the other wives, apportioning to each the work that was for the family. But each woman had her own private property, including horses, and her share of the meat and hides brought in.

There was a big gathering in our lodge that night, men constantly coming in to see the wonderful instrument that could bring down sun fire. It was late when we got to rest. The fire died down. Like the others, I disrobed under the coverings of my couch, and then I went to sleep with never a thought of fear, I, a lone white boy, in a camp of about nine thousand wild Indians!

Lone Walker aroused us soon after daylight the next morning and had me go with him and all his male children to bathe in the stream. Winter and summer the Blackfeet never neglected that daily bath, although sometimes they had to go out and rub themselves with snow, because there was nowhere open water. In winter the women and girls took their baths in sweat lodges.

After the bath we had an early meal of dried meat, roasted before the fire, and small portions of rich, dried buffalo back fat, which was used as the whites use butter.

While we were eating, Lone Walker gave me to understand that his two lodges were needing fresh meat, and that with his son I could go on ahead of the moving camp and kill some. That pleased me; it was just what I was longing to do. You can imagine how much more pleased I was when the great herd of the chief's horses were brought in, and, saying, "You gave me your fire instrument, I now give you something," he selected ten good horses in the herd and said that they were all mine. How rich I felt!

Long before the lodges came down Red Crow and I were riding out along the great south trail. As we topped the slope of the valley and I looked out upon the immense plain ahead, and at the snow-covered peaks of the great mountains bordering it on the west, I said to myself, that this was the happiest day of my life, for I, Hugh Monroe, just a boy, was entering a great section of the country that white men had never traversed!

And, oh, how keen I was to see it all—its plains and stream valleys, its tremendous mountains, its pine-crowned, flat-topped sentinel buttes! Mine was to be the honor of learning their Blackfeet names, and translating them for the map our company was to make for the use of its men.

Also, I looked forward with great desire for the adventures which I felt sure I was to have in that unknown land. Had I known what some of them were to be, I would perhaps have turned right then and made my way back to the safety of the fort.

CHAPTER III
HUNTING WITH RED CROW

When we rode out upon the plain from the valley on our way from the Post we saw several bands of buffaloes away off to the right and left of the trail. Red Crow paid no attention to them, and when, at last, I gave him to understand by signs that I would like to approach the nearest band, a couple of miles ahead and perhaps that far from the trail, he answered that we must do our killing on, or close to, the trail so that the women could put the meat on the pack horses when they came along.

In my hunting back in the forest at home I had learned the value of the saying about the bird in hand, and I thought that we should go after that nearest herd because we might not see another so close to the trail during the day. But I need not have worried; before the day was over I learned that the game of the plains was as ten thousand to one of the game of the Eastern forest.

We rode on perhaps three miles farther, and then, topping one of the many low ridges of the plain, saw an immense herd of buffaloes grazing on the next ridge, and right on the trail. They were slowly moving south, and we waited a long time for the last stragglers of the herd to pass over the ridge and out of sight, and then rode on at an easy lope. As we neared the top of the ridge Red Crow drew his bow from the case and quiver at his back, and then drew out four arrows, three of which he held crosswise in his mouth, fitting the fourth to the bow. I looked into the pan of my gun and made sure that it was full of powder. And then my heart began to beat fast; I was soon to have my first shot at a buffalo! I said to myself: "I must be careful to take good aim! I will not—will not get excited!"

I thought that when near the top of the ridge we would dismount, go on a few steps and cautiously rise up and shoot at the nearest of the buffaloes. But Red Crow never slackened the speed of his horse and I was obliged to follow his lead. Upon reaching the ridge top we saw the great herd resting close under us on the slope, some lying down, others apparently asleep where they stood. But they saw us as soon as we saw them, and away they went, we after them as fast as our eager horses could run.

I had never thought that a horse could be so keen for the chase. Mine just took the bit in his teeth and carried me where he willed. We were soon right at the edge of the frightened herd. I saw Red Crow, some thirty or forty yards ahead of me, ride close up to the right side of an animal and fire an arrow into it, just back of the ribs, and go on without giving it further attention. And then I realized that my horse had brought me close to one of the huge, shaggy-headed, sharp-horned animals, and I poked my gun out and fired, and saw blood almost instantly begin to gush from its nostrils. It made a few more leaps and stopped and fell, and I tried to stop my horse beside it as I shouted, "I have killed a buffalo! I have killed a buffalo!"

But I could not check up the horse, or even turn him, try as I would; a few jumps more and he had me up beside another animal. Then I wished that my pistols were in my belt, instead of in my traveling-kit. I poured a charge of powder from the horn into my hand, but spilled it all before I could get it to the muzzle of my gun. I tried again with the same result. I was not used to loading a gun when riding a horse at its top speed. I gave up the attempt and watched Red Crow, still ahead, and the huge animals thundering along on either side of me. Clumsily built though they were, with deep chest, high hump on the shoulders, and cat hammed, they were far swifter runners than any horse, except for the first few hundred yards of the start. The horse soon tired; they could keep up their killing pace for hours, when frightened. After a half-mile of the chase Red Crow dropped out of it, and I managed to turn my horse with his and start back over the ground that we had come. Ahead of us lay three dead buffaloes, and quite near one was standing humped up, head down, badly wounded. It suddenly dropped and was dead when we rode up to it. I rode on to the one I had killed, eager to examine it, and Red Crow followed me. As we approached it he laughed and gave me to understand that it was an old bull, and therefore no good, its meat too tough to eat, and he pointed to his three, two young cows and a yearling bull, as good, fat meat.

I felt sorry that I had uselessly killed the huge animal. I got down from my horse and examined it. Its massive, sharp-horned, shaggy, and bewhiskered head; its long knee hair, encircling the legs like pantalettes, and the great hump on its shoulders were all very odd. In order to get some idea of its height I lay down on its side, my feet even with its fore feet. Then I reached up and found that I could nowhere near touch the top of its hump. It was between six and seven feet in height!

"One part of it is good," Red Crow signed to me, and got off his horse and skinned down the bull's lower jaw, and pulled out and back the tongue through the opening, cut it off at the base, and handed it to me. I had it that night for my supper, well roasted over the coals, and thought it the best meat I had ever tasted.

I had been wondering how, with nothing but a knife, the hunters managed to butcher such large animals as the buffaloes were. Red Crow now showed me how it was done. We went to the first of his kills, and after withdrawing the arrow, wiping it clean with a wisp of grass, and replacing it in the quiver, he twisted the cow's head sharply around beside the body, the horns sticking into the ground holding it in place. He then grasped the under foreleg by the ankle, and using it as a lever gave a quick heave. Lo, the great body rolled up on its back and remained there propped against the sideways turned head! It was simple enough. He now cut the hide from tail to neck along the belly, and from that in cision down each leg, and then, I helping in the skinning, we soon had the bare carcass lying upon its spread-out hide. Then off came the legs, next the carcass was turned upon its side, an incision was made all along the base of the hump, and it was broken off by hammering the ends of the hump, or dorsal ribs, with a joint of a leg cut off at the knee. Lastly, with a knife and the blows of the leg joint, the ribs were taken off in two sections, and nothing remained upon the hide but a portion of the backbone and the entrails. These we rolled off the hide and the job was done, except tying the portions two by two with strands of the hide, so that they would balance one another on the pack horse.

We had all three animals butchered before the moving camp came up. Then Lone Walker's outfit left the line and came out to us, his head wife supervised the packing of the meat, and we were soon on our way again.

I had had my first buffalo hunt. But I did not know that the buffaloes were to be my staff of life, my food, my shelter, and my clothing, so to speak, for nearly seventy years, until, in fact, they were to be exterminated in the early eighties!

Late in the afternoon of our seventh day out from the fort we went into camp at the junction of two beautiful, clear mountain streams, as I afterward learned, the Belly River, and Old Man's River. The former was so named on account of the broad bend it makes in its course, and the latter because it is believed that Old Man, when making the world, tarried long in the mountains at its head and gambled with Red Old Man, another god. On a mountain-side there is still to be seen a long, smooth furrow in the rock formation, and at the foot of it several huge stone balls which the gods rolled along it at the goal.

The timber along these streams was alive with deer and elk, and from the plains countless herds of buffaloes and antelopes came swarming to them morning and evening to drink. The chiefs decreed that we should camp there for some days for hunting and drying meat, and with Red Crow for my companion I had great sport, killing several of each kind of game. We would ride out in the morning, followed by Red Crow's sister, Su-yi-kai-yi-ah-ki, or Mink Woman, riding a gentle horse and leading a couple of pack horses for bringing in the meat. Of course hundreds of hunters went out each day, but by picketing each evening the horses we were to use next day, and starting very early in the morning, we got a long start of most of them and generally had all the meat we could pack before noon.

We killed buffaloes mostly, for that was the staple meat, meat that one never tired of eating. Antelope, deer, and elk meat was good fresh, for a change, but it did not dry well. As fast as we got the buffalo meat home, Sis-tsi-ah-ki divided it equally in quality and amount among the wives, and they cut it into very thin sheets, and hung it in the sun, and in about two days' time it dried out, and was then packed for transportation in *parflèches*, large rawhide receptacles shaped like an envelope, the flaps laced together.

Su-yi-kai-yi-ah-ki was of great help to us in our hunting. We often sent her into the timber, or around behind a ridge, or up a coulee to drive game to us, and she seldom failed to do it. She was also an expert wielder of the knife, able to skin an animal as quickly as either of us. She was about my age, and tall and slender, quick in all her actions, and very beautiful. Her especial pride was her hair, which she always kept neatly done into two long braids. The ends of them almost touched the ground when she stood up straight. Best of all, she had the same kind heart and happy disposition as her mother, Sis-tsi-ah-ki.

Let me say here that a woman's or girl's name always terminated in "ah-ki," the term for woman. For instance, if a man was named after a bear, he would be called Kyai-yo. If a woman was so named, she would be Kyai-yo-ah-ki (Bear Woman).

From the junction of Belly River and Old Man's River, we trailed southwest across the plain to a large stream that I was told was named Ahk-ai-nus-kwo-na-e-tuk-tai (Gathering-of-Many-Chiefs River), for the reason that in years gone by the chiefs of the Blackfeet tribes had there met the chiefs of tribes living on the west side of the mountains, and concluded a peace treaty with them, which, however, lasted only two summers. We camped beside the river that evening, and the next day, following it up in its deep, wide valley, came to the shore of a large lake from which it ran, and there made camp. Never had I seen so beautiful a lake, or water so clear, and I said so as well as I could in signs and my small knowledge of the language I was trying so hard to learn.

"It is beautiful," Red Crow told me, "but wait until to-morrow; I will then show you a lake far larger and more beautiful.

"We call these the Lakes Inside," he went on. "See, this lake lies partly within the mountains. The one above is wholly within them. But you shall see it all to-morrow."

Over and over I repeated the name for them: Puhkt-o-muk-si-kim-iks (Lakes Inside), until sure that I would not forget it. Now they are known as St. Mary's Lakes.

The morning after we camped at the foot of the lake, Red Crow, his sister, Mink Woman, and I were riding up the east side of the lake soon after daylight, and before any of the hunters were ready to start out. We followed a heavy game trail through quaking aspen groves and across little open, grassy parks, the still water of the lake always in view on our right, and across it the dark, timbered slope running up to a flat-topped mountain ending in an abrupt cliff hundreds of feet in height. We passed a beautiful island close in to our shore, and saw a small band of elk crossing a grassy opening in its heavy timber. Elk and deer, and now and then a few buffaloes, were continually getting out of our way, and once I got a glimpse of a big bull moose as it trotted into a willow thicket, and learned its name from Red Crow's exclamation, "Siks-tsi-so!" But I did not know for some time that the word means "black-going-out-of-sight." A most appropriate name for the shy animal, for generally that is about all that the hunter sees of it, its dark hind quarters disappearing in the thick cover it inhabits.

Passing the head of the lower lake, we crossed a half-mile wide prairie and came to the foot of the upper lake, long, narrow, and running back between mountains rising steeply to great height from the water's edge. I have traveled far; from the St. Lawrence to Hudson's Bay, and from it to the Rockies, and along them south to the Great Salt Lake, but nowhere have I seen anything to equal the beauty of that lake, and the grandeur of its surrounding mountains. I fell in love with the place right then. Red Crow was anxious to go on, but I made him wait until I gazed and gazed at the wonderful scene before me. It was all so beautiful, and yet so stern, that it hurt. Grim, cold, defiant were the rocky heights of the mountains, and blue-black the water of the lake because of its great depth; but for all that I was fascinated by it all. I felt that I would like to camp there a long, long time and climb all those tremendous heights, and explore the whole of the great valley.

"Come!" Red Crow called out at last, and we rode on, crossing the river on a good ford not far below the foot of the lake, and then following another big-game trail through more groves and parks along the west side of the lake. Even here, away back from the plains, were several herds of buffaloes, and more deer and elk trotting and running from our near approach. I was more than once tempted to shoot at one of them, but Red Crow kept signing to me: "Wait! We will kill above here."

At last we arrived at the foot of a long, rocky, and in most places wall-like ridge that ran from the mountains out across the valley and ended in a high cliff jutting out over the lake. We left our horses at the foot of it, followed a game trail up through a break in the wall and came out on the sparsely timbered, rounding top, grass-grown in places. Beyond, the lake, mountain walled, ran back several miles farther. Beyond it a narrow and heavily timbered valley ran away back toward the summit of the range, where reposed long, high belts of what I thought was snow, but later learned was glacial ice, leavings of Cold Maker, the Pi-kun-i say, and his sign that, though the sun has driven him back into the Far North, he will come again with his winds and snows.

We went on a few paces and Red Crow suddenly stopped and pointed to some moving white figures high up on the steep side of a red-rocked mountain ahead and to our right. He made the sign for them: one's forefingers sloping upward and backward from each side of the head above the ears, and by that I knew that they had slender, backward curved horns. "Ai-po-muk-a-kin-a," he called them, meaning "white-big-heads." I had seen a few skins of the animals at the fort, and the factor had told me that they were those of the Rocky Mountain ibex.

"We will go up and kill some of them!" Red Crow said, and we began a climb that lasted for hours. It was my first real mountain climb and I liked it even though I did shiver and sometimes feel faint, when we made our way along the edge of cliffs where a slip of the foot would mean the end for us. We climbed almost straight up and down watercourses; over steep ridges; and then from one rocky, timbered shelf to another, and at last approached the place where we had last seen the animals. Red Crow signed us to be cautious, and with ready bow and arrows led the way across a wide rock shelf, I close at his heels with my gun well primed and cocked, and right at my shoulder his sister, just as eager to see the game as we were. As we neared the edge of the shelf Red Crow motioned us to step up in line with him, and then we all very carefully looked down over it and saw the animals.

But there was something going on with them that made Red Crow motion me to hold still. There were five, all big, white, long-haired males, and all standing at the edge of the shelf just under us, and looking intently at something below that we could not see. Their bodies were much the shape of the buffalo, high over the shoulders, low behind, and very deep chested; and they had long hair pantalettes at the knees, and a long beard. But their heads were very different; long, narrow, flat-faced. Foolish-faced, I thought. Their hair was more of a creamy color than white, and their horns, round, long, slender, curving back to a sharp point, were coal black, as were their eyes, nose, and hoofs. But strangest of all was the attitude of the one on the right of the row; he was sitting down on his haunches, just as a dog or cat sits, as he stared down, and such a position for a hoofed animal, a ruminant, was so odd, so funny, that I almost laughed aloud.

We were not fifty feet above the ibexes, but so intent were they upon what they were watching that they never looked up. Whatever it was, it seemed to be on the shelf of rock just below them and moving to the right, for the ibexes' heads kept turning steadily that way as they watched it. Then presently we saw what it was: another ibex. He came up on the shelf that they were on, a very big, old male, and advanced toward them, and they all turned to face him, backs humped, hair bristling forward, heads lowered, and one advanced, trotting sideways, to meet him. He had also bristled up, and we thought that we were to see a big fight. They met, smelled one another's noses, and leaped into the air, coming down several feet apart, stood motionless for some time, and then the one that belonged to the band went back to his companions while another went forward and through the same performance with the newcomer. It was a very funny sight.

But I was becoming anxious to shoot. I wanted one of the strange animals and was afraid that if we delayed firing they might be come aware of us and suddenly take to flight. I nudged Red Crow and signed him to shoot, and as he raised his bow I aimed at the newcomer, biggest of them all. Twang, went the bow, and whoom, my gun! My animal fell, as did the one Red Crow had chosen for his arrow, and both made faint attempts to regain their feet. The others did not run. Without doubt they had never heard the report of a gun before, and mistook it for the dropping of a time-loosened rock from the heights above. They just stood and stared at their fallen companions, and I drew back from the edge of the shelf and began reloading my gun, while Red Crow continued firing arrow after arrow from the bunch he held in his left hand with the bow. I was not long getting the charge down and pouring priming into the pan, and then I advanced for another shot.

Can you imagine my surprise when I found that I was too late? All the little band were down, dead and dying, and, as I looked, the last of them ceased struggling and lay still! I stared at them, at Red Crow and his bow, and at my gun. In many ways mine was the better weapon, but for running buffaloes, and other quick shooting at short range, I saw that the bow was the thing to use. Right there I determined to get a bow outfit and learn to use it, and always to carry it on my back, and my gun in my hands.

We found a place to get down from our shelf to the dead animals, and I carefully examined mine before skinning it. I found that it had a thick growth of short wool underneath its long, coarse hair, and after that never wondered at the ability of its kind to withstand cold. In winter, the more severe the weather and deep the snow, the higher they range on the mountains, seeking the bare rock which the fierce winds keep free from snow, for there grows their favorite food, moss, and several varieties of lichen.

When I began skinning my kill I was struck by its peculiar odor, just like that of a muskrat and a hundred times as strong. At the rear base of each horn I found a wart-like black gland filled with yellowish, greasy musk. When I finished skinning my animal I began on another, and we soon had them all skinned. I then took the boss, or dorsal ribs, of my kill and wrapped them in the two hides I was to carry, although Red Crow and his sister laughed at me, and gave me to understand that the meat was not good. I confess that I did not enjoy it. It was coarse and tough, and musky. However, a young, fat male or female of this high mountain species is good eating—when no other kind of meat is obtainable.

While we were preparing to leave the shelf I saw my first bighorns, a band of ewes and young between us and the lake, and five big rams on the mountain-side to the south of us. We had no time to go after them, as the sun was getting low, and anyhow I was well satisfied with our success of the day. We hurried down the mountain to our horses and started on the long trail to camp. Whenever we crossed a park and looked out upon the lake we saw its calm surface broken by the jumping of hundreds of fish, some of the splashes undoubtedly made by fish of great size. I afterward found that they were the so-called Mackinaw trout, running in weight up to forty pounds. Besides them these lakes are full of cutthroat trout, and what the whites call Dolly Varden trout, and whitefish.

The sun had set when we crossed the river and the big prairie at the foot of the upper lake, and started on the trail along the lower lake. It was almost dark when, hurrying along at a good lope, we crossed the park opposite the island, and entered a quaking aspen grove. And then, without warning, Red Crow's horse gave a sudden sideways leap and threw him, and went snorting and tearing off to the right, and Mink Woman's and my horses took after him, plunging and kicking with fright, and try as we would we could not stop them. I saw the girl knocked from her horse by a projecting, low bough of a cottonwood tree. Behind us Red Crow was shouting "Kyai-yo! Kyai-yo! Spom-ok-it!" (A bear! A bear! Help!)

As I could not stop my horse I sprang off him, holding fast to my gun, passed Mink Woman struggling to her feet, and ran to assist my friend, his continued cries for help almost drowned by the terrible roars of an angry bear. Never had I heard anything so terrible. It struck fear to my heart. I wanted to turn and run from it, but I just couldn't! And there close behind me came the girl, crying, "Spom-os! Spom-os!" (Help him! Help him!) I just gritted my teeth and kept on.

CHAPTER   IV
A FIGHT WITH THE RIVER PEOPLE

I went but a little way through the brush when, in the dim light, I saw Red Crow clinging with both hands to a slender, swaying, quaking aspen, and jerking up his feet from the up-reaching swipes of a big bear's claws. He could find no lodgment for his feet and could climb no higher; as it was, the little tree threatened to snap in two at any moment. It was bending more and more to the right, and directly over the bear, and he was lifting his legs higher and higher. There was no time to be lost! Scared though I was, I raised my gun, took careful sight for a heart shot at the big animal, and pulled the trigger. Whoom! And the bear gave a louder roar than ever, fell and clawed at its side, then rose and came after me, and as I turned to run I saw the little tree snap in two and Red Crow drop to the ground.

I turned only to bump heavily into Mink Woman, and we fell, both yelling, and sprang up and ran for our lives, expecting that every jump would be our last. But we had gone only a short way when it struck me that we were not being pursued, and then, oh, how can I describe the relief I felt when I heard Red Crow shout to us: "Puk-si-put! Ahk-ai-ni!" (Come! He is dead!)

Well, when I heard that my strength seemed suddenly to go from me, and I guess that the girl felt the same way. We turned back, hand in hand, wabbly on our legs, and gasping as we recovered our breath. Again and again Red Crow called to us, and at last I got enough wind into me to answer him, and he came to meet us, and led us back to the bear.

I had not thought that a grizzly could be as big as it was. It lay there on its side as big bodied as a buffalo cow. The big mouth was open, exposing upper and lower yellow fangs as long as my forefinger. I lifted up one huge forefoot and saw that the claws were four inches and more in length. Lastly, I saw that there was an arrow deep in its breast. Then, as we stood there, Red Crow made me understand that when his horse threw him and he got to his feet, he found the bear standing erect facing him, and he had fired an arrow into it and taken to the nearest tree. I knew the rest. I saw that the arrow had pierced the bear's lungs; that it would have bled to death anyhow. But my shot had been a heart shot, and just in time, for the little tree was bending, breaking even as I fired, and the bear would have had Red Crow had it not started in pursuit of us.

"The claws, you take them!" Red Crow now signed to me. But I refused. I knew how highly they were valued for necklace ornaments, and I wanted no necklace. Nor did I want the great hide, for its new coat was short, and the old winter coat still clung to it in faded yellow patches. Red Crow quickly unjointed the long fore claws, and we hunted around and found our ibex hides, which had come to the ground with us, and resumed our way in the gathering night. The horses had, of course, gone on, and would never stop until they found the band in which they belonged.

After the experience we had had, we went on with fear in our hearts, imagining that every animal we heard moving was a bear. There was no moon, and in the thick groves we had to just feel our way. But at last we passed the foot of the lake and saw the yellow gleaming of the hundreds of lodges of the camp on the far side of the river. The ford was too deep, the water too swift for us to cross it on foot, so we called for help, and several who heard came over on horseback and took us up behind, and across to the camp, where we found Lone Walker was gathering a party to go in search for us.

What a welcome we got! The women hugged and kissed Red Crow and his sister, and me too, just as if I were another son, and Lone Walker patted us on the shoulder and followed us into the lodge, and fussed at the women to hurry and set food before us. We ate, and let Mink Woman tell the story of the day, which she did between bites, and oh, how her eyes flashed and the words poured out as she described with telling gestures our experience with the bear! A crowd of chiefs and warriors had come into the lodge when word went around that we had killed a big bear, and listened to her story with close attention and many exclamations of surprise and approval; and when she ended, and Red Crow had exhibited the huge claws, Lone Walker made a little speech to me. I understood enough of it, with his signs, to know that he praised me for my bravery in going to his son's rescue and giving the bear its death shot.

Let me say here that in those days, with only bow and arrows, or a flintlock gun, the bravest of hunters generally let the grizzly alone if he would only let them alone. The trouble was that the grizzly, sure of his terrible strength, only too often charged the hunter at sight and without the slightest provocation. I have recently read Lewis and Clark's "Journal," and find that they agree with me that the grizzly, or as they called it, the white bear, was a most ferocious and dangerous animal.

The chiefs having decided that camp should not be moved until the next day, Red Crow and his sister took me next morning up a stream now called Swift Water, running into the river from the west. There were a number of lakes upon it, and one of them, just above a falls, was a very beautiful sheet of water. Beyond it, at what was the head of the main fork of the stream, were more great deposits of ice, old Cold Maker's leavings. But I was not so much interested in them as I was in taking note of the beaver signs, which was a part of my duty on this trip of discovery into the southland. It was the factor's intention to send some *engagés* trappers into it if I found enough fur to keep them busy. Between this lake and a smaller one lying at the foot of a great ice sheet, I found no less than thirteen dammed ponds, all containing a number of in habited beaver houses; and there were a number of their ponds farther down the stream.

Camp was broken the following morning, but before the lodges came down I was off on the trail with the chiefs. We topped the long, high ridge sloping up eastward from the lower lake, and looked out upon the greatest expanse of mountain- and butte-studded plains that I had ever seen. And I thrilled at the thought that I was the very first one of my race to see it. Lone Walker pointed down to a small stream heading in a great patch of pine and spruce on the side of the ridge.

"That is the Little River. Far to the east it joins the Big River of the South," he told me, and I realized that I was on top of the watershed of the Gulf of Mexico. We rode on down to the stream and I got off my horse and drank from it for good luck. The whites misnamed it when they, years afterward, called it Milk River. The Blackfoot name was best, for it is a very small river for all its three hundred and more miles of length from its source to its junction with the Missouri.

As I drank the swamp-flavored water I thought how fine it would be to make a dugout there, and voyage down the stream to the Missouri, and down that to the Mississippi, and thence to the Gulf of Mexico and its tropical shores. What a long journey it would be; thousands of miles! What strange peoples I should see; tribe after tribe of Indians, then Americans, and at last the French and the Spanish of the Far South! And what adventure there would be! Fights with some of those wild tribes, and with bears, and perhaps with lawless whites. They would try to take from me the hundreds of beaver pelts that I should trap on the way! But no! My dugout would not carry many skins, and if I survived the dangers I should arrive, poor and ragged, among a strange people, and have to work for them for a few pence a day. "Away with you, dream," I said, and mounted my horse and rejoined the chiefs.

Coming to the southernmost little branch of the south fork of the river, Lone Walker, in the lead, got down from his horse, examined some tracks in the mud, and called out something which caused the others to spring from their horses and crowd around him. So did I, and saw several fresh moccasin tracks. At sight of them the chiefs had all become greatly excited, and talked so fast that I could understand nothing of what they said. I concluded, however, that the tracks had been made by some enemy, and saw by closer examination that the makers of them had worn soft, leather-soled moccasins, very different from the *parflèche* or semi-rawhide soles of all Blackfoot summer footwear.

Looking back on our trail, and seeing a large body of warriors coming to take the lead, several of the chiefs signaled them to hurry; and when they rode up Lone Walker gave some orders that sent them scurrying off in all directions. One of them presently came back in sight from the timber above the crossing, and signed to us to come to him. We all mounted and went up, and he led us into the timber and to a camping-ground where many lodges, several hundred, I thought, had recently been pitched. Several of the chiefs poked out the ashes of one or two fireplaces and uncovered red coals; it was evident that the campers had moved away the day before.

The chiefs were greatly excited over the find, and after a short council hurried back to the trail and gave orders that we should go into camp right there. While we waited for the long column to come up I gave Lone Walker the query sign—holding my hand up in front of me, palm outward, and waving it like the inverted pendulum of a clock, and he answered in speech and signs both, so that I understood: "The campers here were River People. We have forbidden them to come over here on our plains, but they keep coming and stealing our buffaloes. We shall now make them cry!"

"You are going to fight them?" I signed.

"Yes."

A queer feeling came over me at his answer. I shivered. In my mind's eye I saw a great battle, arrows flying and guns booming, and men falling and crying out in their death agony. And for what? Just a few of the buffaloes that blackened the plains!

"Don't fight! There are plenty of buffaloes! Let the River People go in peace with what few they have killed," I signed, but he gave me no answer other than a grim smile, and rode out to meet the head of the column.

Word had already gone back the whole length of it of our discovery, and as the excited people came up to their allotted place in the great circle and slung the packs from their horses, the women chattering and the men urging them to hurry and get out their war clothes, dogs barking and horses calling to one another, the din of it all was deafening.

I now learned that, when there was time for the change, the warriors put on their war clothes before going against the enemy. The change was soon made, and it was startling. Somber, everyday, plain wear had given place to shirts beautifully embroidered with porcupine-quill work of bright colors and pleasing design, and fringed with white weasel skins and here and there scalps of the enemy. The leggings were also fringed, and generally painted with figures of medicine animals. Not a few wore moccasins of solid quill embroidery. Every man had on a war bonnet of eagle tail feathers, or horns and weasel skins, and carried suspended from his left arm a thick, round shield of shrunk bull hide, from the circumference of which eagle tail feathers fluttered gayly in the wind. Thus dressed, with bow and arrow case on their backs, guns in hand, and mounted on their prancing, high-spirited horses, the hundreds of warriors who soon gathered around us presented the most picturesque and at the same time formidable sight that I had ever seen. I admired them, and yet they filled me with terror against them; if they chose to attack us, our fort, our cannon and guns were as a barrier of feathers against the wind! And I, just a boy, was alone with them! I shivered. And then Lone Walker spoke kindly to me, and my fear died before his smile.

"Come! We go! You shall see something to make your heart glad!" he said.

I hesitated, and the warriors suddenly broke out into a song that I knew must be a song of battle. It thrilled me; excited me. I sprang upon my horse and we were off. Lone Walker signed to me to fall in behind, and I found myself riding beside Red Crow at the rear of the swiftly moving band. Following the trail of the enemy we soon topped a long, brushy slope and turned down into a beautiful timbered valley, and up it along a broad, clear stream in which I saw many a trout leaping for flies, and which, from the signs, was alive with beavers. It was the Pu-nak-ik-si, or Cutbank River, so named on account of the rock walls on both sides of the lower part of its valley.

Three or four miles above where we struck the valley it narrowed rapidly, hemmed in by the mountains, and we had to slow up, for the narrow trail led on through a thick growth of timber and, in places, almost impenetrable brush. Then, for a short distance below the forks, the valley widened again, and there we passed the largest beaver dam that I had ever seen. It ran for all of a half-mile from slope to slope across the valley, forming a pond of hundreds of acres in extent, that was dotted with the lodges of the bark eaters. Above it we turned up the south fork of the stream and neared the summit of the range. The valley narrowed to a width of a few hundred yards; ahead a high rock wall crossed it, and the trail ran steeply up the right mountain-side to gain its rough top. We were a long time making that for we were obliged to ride in single file because of the narrowness of the trail. The chiefs, leading, raised a great shout when they reached the edge of the wall, and signed back that they could see the enemy. We crowded on as fast as we could, Red Crow and I the last to top the wall, and oh, how anxious I was to see what was ahead!

I saw, and just held my horse and stared and stared. For a mile or more from the wall the trail still ran south up a rocky slope, then turned, and, still rising, ran along a very steep slope to the summit of the range. Along that slope the trail was black with riders and loose horses, hurrying across it at a trot and in single file, and back at the turn of the trail the rear guard of the fleeing tribe was making a stand against our advance. The warriors were afoot, their horses having gone on with the column, and our men had left their horses and were running on and spreading out, those who had guns already beginning to use them.

"Come on! Hurry!" Red Crow shouted to me, and was off. I did not follow him, not at first, but as the River People's guard retreated and our men advanced, I did ride on, dreading to see men fall, but withal so fascinated by the fight that I could not remain where I was. I went to the spot where the enemy had first made their stand, and saw several bodies lying among the rocks. They had already been scalped.

The last of the camp movers, the men, women, and children with the pack and loose horses, had all now crossed the long, steep slope, the latter part of which was very steep, and ran down to the edge of a cut-walled chasm of tremendous depth, and had gone out of sight beyond the summit. The guards were now on the trail along this most dangerous part of it, our warriors following them in single file at long bow range, but all of them except two or three in the lead, unable to use their weapons.

It was a duel between these and the two or three rear men of the enemy. Our lead man was, as I afterward learned, Lone Walker, and the men next to him Chiefs Bear Head and Bull-Turns-Around. All three had guns and were firing and reloading them and firing again as fast as they could, and doing terrible execution. One after another I saw five of the enemy fall from the trail, which was just a narrow path in the slide rock, and go bouncing and whirling down, and off the edge of that great cliff into space. It was a terrible sight! It made me tremble! I strained my body as I sat there on my horse, scrouged down as each one fell.

I could not see that any of our warriors were falling; they were keeping themselves pretty well protected with their shields. Capping the slope where all this was going on was a long, narrow wall of rock running out from the summit of the range, and happening to glance up at it I saw numbers of the enemy hurrying out along it to get opposite our men and shoot down at them. I instantly urged my horse forward, shouting as loud as I could, but no one looked back and I knew that I was not heard. I went on to where the horses had been left, jumped from mine there and ran on out along the slope, shouting again and pointing up to the top of the rock wall. At last some one saw me, and gave the alarm, and the whole party stopped and looked at me, then up where I was pointing and saw their danger, and all turned and started to retreat.

But they had no more than started than the enemy began firing down at them. It was a long way down, several hundred yards, and their arrows and the few balls they fired did no damage; and seeing that, one of the enemy toppled a boulder off the cliff. It struck the slope with a loud crash and rolled and bounded on almost as swiftly as a ball from a gun, and I expected it to hurl three or four of our running men off the trail and down over the edge of the cliff. But when within twenty or thirty feet of the line it bounded high from the slope and shot out away over the trail, and away out over the cliff, and long afterward I heard it crash onto the bottom of the chasm.

Now the enemy abandoned their weapons and began, all of them, to hurl boulders down onto the slope. Had they done that at first they would likely have swept many of our men off the trail and over the cliff; but now the most of them had passed the danger line. As the last of them were running out from under the outer point of the wall, a man there loosed a last big rock; it broke into many pieces when it hit the slope, and these went hurtling down with tremendous speed. There was no possibility of dodging them; two men were struck; one of them rolled down to the cliff and off it, but the other, the very last in the line, was whirled around, and as he dropped, half on and half off the trail, the man next to him turned back and helped him to his feet, and without further assistance he staggered on to safety. He was Lone Walker. His right shoulder was broken and terribly bruised. The man we had lost was Short Arrow, young, just recently made a warrior.

We all gathered where the horses had been left, and a doctor man bound the chief's wound as best he could. There was much talk of Short Arrow's sudden going, and regret for it; and there was rejoicing, too; the enemy had paid dearly, seven lives, for what buffalo and other game they had killed out on the Blackfeet plains.

The sun was setting. As we tightened saddle cinches and prepared to go, we had a last look out along the slope. A great crowd of people was gathered on the summit watching us, and up on the wall top over the trail, sharply outlined against the sunset sky, dozens of warriors were gathering piles of rocks to hurl down at us should we again attempt to cross the slope. Our chiefs had no thought of it. The enemy had been sufficiently punished, and anyhow the stand that they had taken was unassailable. We got onto our horses and hurried to get down into the valley below the rock wall while there was still a little light, and from there on let the horses take us home.

We arrived in camp long after midnight. The people were still up, awaiting our return, and the greeting that we got surprised me. The women and old men gathered around us, shouting the names of the warriors, praising them for their bravery, and giving thanks to the gods for their safe return. But there was mourning too; when the noise of the greeting subsided we could hear the relatives of Short Arrow wailing over their loss.

I did not sleep much that night; every time I fell into a doze I saw the bodies of the enemy bounding down that rocky slope and off the edge of the thousand foot wall, and awoke with a start.

Although suffering great pain in his shoulder, Lone Walker the next morning declared that he was able to travel, and camp was soon broken. After crossing the valley of Cutbank River we left the big south trail, turning off from it to the southeast, and after a time striking the valley of another stream, the Nat-ok-i-o-kan, or Two-Medicine-Lodge River. I learned that this was the main fork of Kyai-is-i-sak-ta, or Bear River, the stream which Lewis and Clark had named Maria's River, after the sweetheart of one of them. But I did not know that for many a year after I first saw it.

We went into camp in a heavily timbered bottom walled on the north side by a long, high cliff, at the foot of which was a great corral in the shape of a half circle, the cliff itself forming the back part of it. It was built of fallen trees, driftwood from the river, and boulders, and was very high and strong. Red Crow told me that it was a buffalo trap; that whole herds of buffaloes were driven off the cliff into it. I could not understand much of what he told me, but later on saw a great herd decoyed to a cliff and stampeded over it, a waterfall of huge, brown, whirling animals. It was a wonderful spectacle. I shall have something to say about that later on.

I now learned that we had come to this particular camping place for the purpose of building a great lodge offering, called o-kan, or his dream, to the sun. When we went into camp the lodges were not put up in the usual formation, but were set to form a great circle on the level, grassy bottom between the timber, bordering the stream, and the cliff. In the center of this circle, the sacred lodge was to be erected with ceremonies that would last for some days.

On the following morning Red Crow and I, Mink Woman accompanying us, went hunting; we were to bring in enough meat to last our two lodges until the great festival ended. As usual, we started out very early, long before the great majority of the hunters were up. We rode down the valley through a number of bottoms of varying size, seeing a few deer, a band of antelopes, and two or three elk, but finding no buffaloes until we neared the junction of the river with another stream, which Red Crow told me was Mi-sin-ski-is-i-sak-ta (Striped-Face—or, in other words, Badger River). There, on the point between the two streams, we discovered a large herd of buffaloes filing down into the bottom to drink. We hurried on through the timber to get ahead of them, intending to hide in the brush on the point of land between the streams and dash into them when they came near. But as buffaloes often did, they suddenly broke into a run when part way down the slope, their thirst and sight of the water urging them forward, so we crossed the river, and riding in the shelter of the willows made our approach. They had all crowded out on the narrow point of land ahead and were drinking from both streams.

"We will kill many!" Red Crow signed to me as we rode through the willows, and then out from the stream in the shelter of some clumps of berry brush, through which we could glimpse the solidly packed rows of the drinking animals. That was my thought, too, for I saw that we could get within fifty or sixty yards of them before they discovered our approach. I loosed the pistols in my belt, and slipped the case from my gun as we made our way into the last piece of brush; when we went out of it, Red Crow signed to me, we were to charge. Just then a gun boomed somewhere ahead of us, and at the report the buffaloes whirled out from the streams and with a thunder and rattle of hoofs came straight toward us, a solid mass of several hundred head that covered the width of the point. Red Crow yelled something to us, but we could not hear him. We all turned about, the girl letting go the two horses she was leading, and fled. Unless our horses could outrun the stampede they were sure to be gored, and down we would go to a terrible death!

CHAPTER V
BUFFALO HUNTING

When we cleared that brush patch I looked back. The buffaloes were no more than fifty yards behind us and the brush was gone, trampled down to its roots. I did not see the two horses that Mink Woman had been leading, or think of them at that time; my one thought was to get away from that onrushing wall of shaggy, sharp-horned, bobbing heads. Red Crow, frantically thumping his horse with his heels, was leading us, heading obliquely toward Badger River, and waving to us to follow him. Mink Woman was just ahead of me, but she had the slower horse and I was gaining upon her, even as the buffaloes were gaining upon us all. I wondered if we could possibly clear their front. I rode up beside the girl, on her left, and hung there to protect her as best I could. Nearer and nearer came the buffaloes. When they werewithin fifty feet of us, and we still fifty or sixty yards from the river, I fired my gun at them and to my surprise dropped a big cow. But that had no effect upon the others; they surged on over her body as though it were no more than an ant hill.

"I must try again!" I said to myself and holding gun and bridle in my right hand, drew a pistol with my left. It was to be my last shot, and I held it as long as I could. We neared the river; the herd kept gaining upon us, came up to us and I leaned out and fired straight at a big head that I could almost touch with the muzzle of the pistol. It dropped. Looking ahead then I saw that we were close to the edge of a high cutbank at the edge of the river, saw Red Crow leap his horse from it and go out of sight; a couple more jumps of our horses and we, too, would clear it. But just then a big head thumped into the side of my horse, knocking him against Mink Woman's horse. As I felt him falling with me I let go pistol and gun and bridle, and reaching out blindly grasped the mane of her horse with both hands and swung free. The next instant another big head struck her horse a mighty thud in the flank and whirled him half around and off the cutbank, and down we went with a splash into deep water; we were safe!

I let go the horse, and the girl, still on its back, swam it downstream to shallow water, I following, and we finally passed below the cutbank and went ashore on the point, Red Crow going out a little ahead of us. A man skinning a buffalo there whirled around and stared at us open-mouthed, and then cried: "What has happened to you?"

"You did it, you stampeded the buffaloes onto us! We have had a narrow escape!" Red Crow answered.

But my one thought now was of my gun and pistol; I ran on to find them, dreading to see them trampled into useless pieces of wood and iron, and the hunter mounted his horse and came with the others after me.

It was a couple of hundred yards up to where we had made our sudden turn, and there in the trampled and broken brush patch we found the two pack horses, frightfully gored and trampled, both dead. Mink Woman had led them by a single, strong rawhide rope, and the buffaloes striking it had dragged them, gored them, knocked them off their feet.

We went on, past the first buffalo that I had killed, and soon came to the other one, and just beyond it to my horse, disemboweled, down, and dying. Red Crow put an arrow into him and ended his misery. Just in front of him lay my gun, and I gave a shout of joy when I saw that it had not been trampled. We could not find the pistol, and it occurred to me that it might be under the dead horse; we turned him over and there it was, pressed hard into the ground but unbroken! We looked at one another and laughed, and Red Crow sang the "I Don't Care" song—I did not know it then—and the hunter said: "All is well! You have lost horses, they are nothing. You are wet, your clothes will dry. You have two fat buffaloes, be glad!"

And at that we laughed again. But I guess that my laugh had a little shake in it; I kept seeing that terrible wall of frightened buffaloes thundering out upon us!

The first thing that I did was to reload my gun and recovered pistol, and draw the wet charge and reload it. Then Mink Woman and I turned to our two buffaloes and Red Crow hurried home for horses to replace those that we had lost. It was late afternoon when we got into camp with our loads of meat. So ended another experience in my early life on the plains.

During the following days of our encampment there on the Two Medicine, the whole time was given over to the ceremonies of the o-kan, or medicine lodge, as our company men came to call it, and I was surprised to learn by it how intensely religious these people were, and how sincerely they reverenced and honored their gods. My greatest surprise came at the start, when I learned that it was women, not men, who had vowed to build the great lodge to the sun, the men merely assisting them. It was then, too, that I got my first insight into the important position of women in the tribe; they were far from being the slaves and drudges that I had been told they were.

During the year that had passed a number of women had vowed to the sun to build this sacrifice to him if he would cure some loved relative of his illness, or bring him safely home from the war trail, and those whose prayers were granted now banded together, under the lead of the most experienced one of their number, to fulfill their vows. The different ceremonies were very intricate, and to me, with my slight knowledge of the language, quite mysterious. But, Christian though I was, I was completely carried away by them, and took part in some of them as I was told to do by Lone Walker and his family.

On the day after the great lodge was put up, Red Crow's mother took him and Mink Woman and me into it, and had one of the medicine women give us each a small piece of the sacred dried buffalo tongues which were being handed to all the people as they came in for them. I held mine, watching what the others did with theirs, and then, when my turn came, I held it up to the sky and made a little prayer to the sun for good health, long life, and happiness, and having said that, I buried a part of the meat in the ground, at the same time crying out: "Hai-yu! Sak-wi-ah-ki, kim-o-ket!" (Oh, you! Earth Mother, pity me!)

After that was done the mother and Red Crow and his sister made sacrifices to the sun, giving a beautifully embroidered robe, a bone necklace, and a war bonnet, which a medicine man hung to the roof poles while they prayed. But I was not forgotten; the good mother handed me a pair of new, embroidered moccasins and told me to hand them to the medicine man to hang up, and prayed for me while he did so. I could not understand half of it, but enough to know that in her I had a true friend, a second mother as it were.

On the following day I learned that I had a second father, too. The warriors, gathered in front of the great lodge, were one by one counting their coups, their deeds of bravery, with the aid of friends enacting each scene of battle, and showing just how they had conquered the enemy. It was all like a play; a very interesting play. As Red Crow and I stood at the edge of the crowd looking on, Lone Walker saw us, raised his hand for silence, and said loudly, so that all could hear: "There stand my two sons, my red son and my white son. Come, son Red Crow, count coups for yourself and your brother, too, as he cannot yet speak our language well."

At that Red Crow took my hand and we walked out in front of the chief, turned and faced the crowd, and then Red Crow described how we had killed the big grizzly, I going to his rescue and giving it the death shot just in time to save him. He ended, and the drummers stationed beside the chiefs banged their drums, and the people shouted their approval. Following that, Lone Walker again addressed the crowd: "By that brave deed which you have heard, my white son has earned a name for himself," he said. "It was a brave deed; by his quick rush in and timely shot he saved my red son's life, and so he must have a brave and good man's name. I give him the name of one who has recently gone from us in his old age. Look at him, all of you, my son, Rising Wolf!"

And at that the people again shouted approval, and the drummers banged their drums. Of course I did not know then all that he had said, but I did know that I had been named Mah-kwi-i-po-ats (Wolf Rising, or, as the whites prefer to translate it, Rising Wolf).

The preparations for building the o-kan required two days' time; the attendant ceremonies four days more, four, the sacred number, the number of the world directions, north, south, east, and west. On the morning following the last day of the ceremonies we broke camp and, leaving the great lodge and its wealth of sun offerings to the elements, moved south again, or, rather, southwest, in order to regain the mountain trail. Their religious duties fulfilled, the people were very happy, and I felt as light-hearted as any of them, and eager to see more—see all of their great country.

We crossed Badger River, and then Sik-o-kin-is-i-sak-ta, or Black Barkbirch River, and encamped on a small stream named O-saks-i-i-tuk-tai, Back Fat, or as our French*voyageurs* later translated it, Depouille Creek. From there our next camp was on Kok-sis-tuk-wi-a-tuk-tai (Point-of-Rocks River). I never knew why the whites named it Sun River. Nor did I dream that the day was to come when I would see its broad bottoms fenced in and irrigated, and a fort built upon it to house blue-coated American soldiers. If I then gave the future any thought, it was that those great plains and mountains would ever be the hunting-ground of the Black feet, and the unfailing source of a great supply of furs for our company.

We camped on this stream well out from the mountains, and the next morning, moving on, at noon arrived at its junction with a great river which at first sight I knew must be the Missouri, the O-muk-at-ai of the Blackfeet tribes. Below, not far away by the sound, I could hear the dull roar of a waterfall. We turned downstream, crossed on a swift and fairly deep ford above the falls, and went into camp. As soon as the lodges were up and the women had cooked some meat for us, Red Crow and I saddled fresh horses and struck out to see the country. We had come to the trail of Lewis and Clark, and I was anxious to learn if they had had any followers, if the American Fur Company's men had come into the country, as my factor feared.

We rode to the fall, and after looking at it moved on down and came upon an old and very dim trail along which lay here and there log cuttings about eight feet long and a foot or more in diameter. They were well worn; small pieces of rock and gravel were embedded in them, and I saw at once that they had been used for rollers under boats in portaging them around the falls. I realized how great a task that had been when Red Crow guided me down to all the falls, the last a number of miles below our camp. The Blackfoot name for the falls is I-pum-is-tuk-wi (Rock-Wall-across-the-River.)

Sitting on the shore of the river below the last falls, at the point where the portage had begun, I tried to get some information from Red Crow as to the white men who had passed up there, but he could tell me nothing. As we talked I was idly heaping a pile of sand before me, and in doing so uncovered two long, rusty spikes.

"What a find! What a rich find! Give me one of them," Red Crow exclaimed, and I handed him one.

"See! It is long. It will make two arrow points," he explained. And at that I carefully pocketed mine. Material for arrowheads, iron, I mean, was very valuable at that time, in that country. Our company was selling arrow points of hoop iron at the rate of a beaver skin for six points. Some of the Blackfeet hunters were still using flint points which they made themselves.

And that reminds me of something. At the foot of the buffalo trap cliffs on the Two Medicine I picked up one evening a number of flint and obsidian arrow points, many of them perfectly and beautifully fashioned. I took them to the lodge and offered them to Lone Walker, thinking that I was doing him a good turn. But he started back from them as though they had been a rattlesnake, and refused to even touch them. "Some of those, especially the black ones, are surely Crow points, and so unlucky to us," he explained. "This was Crow country. We took it from them. Maybe our fathers killed the owners of those points. But the shadows of the dead keep coming back to watch their property, and cause sickness, trouble, to any who take it. I wish that you would take the points back where you got them and leave them there."

I did so, but carefully cached them under a rock, and years later recovered them. But that is not all. After returning to the lodge I asked Lone Walker where the people obtained the black, as they called it, ice rock for making their arrows, and he told me that away to the south, near the head of Elk River, or in other words, the Yellowstone, were springs of boiling water, some of them shooting high in the air with tremendous roaring, and that near one of these springs was a whole butte of the ice rock, and it was there that his people went to get their supply. "But it is a dreadful place!" he concluded. "We approach it with fear in our hearts, and make great sacrifices to the gods to protect us. And as soon as we arrive at the ice rock butte we snatch up what we need of it and hurry away."

He was telling me, of course, of the wonderful geysers of the Yellowstone. I believe that I am the first white person who ever heard of them.

But to continue: When Red Crow and I returned home that evening, I asked Lone Walker if his people had seen the white men who had left the cut logs in the trail around the falls, and he replied that neither the Pi-kun-i, nor any other of the Blackfeet tribes had seen them, but he himself had heard of them from the Earth House People—the Mandans—when visiting them several summers back. They had been a large party, traveling in boats, had wintered with the Mandans and gone westward, even to the Everywheres-water of the west, and the next summer had come back, this time on horses instead of in boats. If you have read Lewis and Clark's "Journal," you will remember that they met and fought—on what must have been Cutbank River—some people that they thought were Blackfeet. They were not. They must have been a war party of Crows or some other tribe going through the country.

I next asked Lone Walker if he had ever seen white men on the Missouri River waters.

"Two. In the Mandan camp. Of a race the Mandans call Nothing White Men," he answered.

And from that time the Blackfoot name for the French has been Kis-tap-ap-i-kwaks (Useless, or Nothing White Men), as distinguishing them from the English, the Red Coats, and the Americans, Long Knives.

Lone Walker's answer pleased me; it was evident that the American Fur Company had not entered the Blackfoot, or even the Mandan country, far below. But even then that company was pushing, pushing its forts farther and farther up the Missouri, and the day was coming, far off but coming, when I would be one of its employees!

We camped there at the falls several days and hunted buffaloes, making several big runs and killing all the meat that was wanted at that time. Our lodges were pitched close to the river, right where the whites are now building the town they have named Great Falls.

Our next move was out to the point of the little spur of the mountains that is named Highwood. Its slopes were just alive with deer and elk, especially elk, and Red Crow and I killed two of them, big fat bulls, for a change of meat for our lodges. We did all the hunting for Lone Walker's big family; they required an awful lot of meat; of fresh meat about three pounds a day for each person, and each day there were also a number of guests to be fed. At a rough guess I put the amount that we used at three hundred pounds a day. Do you wonder that Red Crow and I, and Mink Woman helping us, were kept pretty busy?

Leaving the Highwood we moved out to Arrow River (Ap-si-is-i-sak-ta), and once more I felt that I was in country that white men had never seen. The Arrow River valley is for most of its course a deep, walled gash in the plains; there are long stretches of it where neither man nor any animal, except the bighorn, can climb its red rock cliffs. But the moment I first set eyes upon it, I liked it. I always did like cliffs, their ledges, and caves hiding one can never tell what mysteries. There were many bighorn along these cliffs, and mule deer were plentiful in all the rough breaks of the valley. Out on the plains endless herds of buffaloes and antelopes grazed, coming daily down steep and narrow, deep-worn trails to drink at the river; and in the valley itself every patch of timber fringing the stream sheltered white-tailed deer and elk. There were many beavers, pond beavers and bank beavers, along the stream. Bear tracks were everywhere to be seen, in the dusty game trails, and in the river shore sands.

We wound down into the deep canyon by following a well-worn game trail down a coulee several miles in length, and when we went into camp between a fine cottonwood grove and the stream, and Lone Walker said that we would remain there for some time, I was much pleased, for I wanted to do a lot of hunting and exploring along the cliffs with Red Crow.

We could not do it the next day, for we had to get meat for the two lodges. That was not difficult. With Mink Woman to help us, and leading six pack horses, we left very early in the morning and rode down the valley for four or five miles, examining the many game trails that came into the valley; there was one in every break, every coulee cutting the rock wall formation. We at last struck a well-worn trail that came into the valley through a gap in the cliff not twenty feet wide, and under a projecting rock shelf about ten feet high. We saw that we could climb onto the shelf, and shoot straight down at the game as it passed, so Red Crow rode up the trail to look out on the plain and learn if it would pay us to make our stand there. He was gone a long time, and when he returned said that a very large herd of buffaloes was out beyond the head of the coulee, and slowly grazing toward it; he thought that it would be coming in to water before noon. We therefore hid our horses in some timber below the mouth of the coulee, and then all three climbed up on the rock shelf and sat down. I held my gun ready, laid a pistol on either side of me, and Red Crow strung his bow and got out a handful of arrows.

It was hot there on that shelf. The sun blazed down upon us, and we could not have held out had not a light wind been blowing down the coulee. It was past noon when a most peculiar noise came to us with the wind; a deep, roaring noise like distant, but steady thunder. I asked what caused it.

"It is the bulls; the buffalo bulls are grunting because now is their mating season," Red Crow explained. "They now take wives. They are very mad; they fight one another, and night and day keep up that grunting."

The noise became louder and louder. "They come. They are coming now to drink," said Red Crow, and soon after that we saw the lead of the herd coming around a bend in the coulee. A number of bulls came first, heads down, and swaying as they walked with ponderous tread, and as they came nearer I saw that they were making that peculiar noise with their mouths closed, or all but closed. It was what I called a grunting bellow, very deep sounding, long sustained, a sound wholly unlike any other sound in the world. It was a sound that exactly fitted the animal that made it. As the buffalo's appearance was ever that of a forbidding, melancholy animal brooding over strange mysteries, so was its close-mouthed bellowing expressive of great sadness, and unfathomable mystery; of age-old mysteries that man can never penetrate. Often, as we gazed at bulls standing on some high point, and as motionless as though of stone, Indians have said to me: "They know! They know everything, they see everything! Nothing has been hidden from them from the time Old Man made the world and put them upon it!"

Perhaps so! Let us not be too sure that we are the only wise ones that roam this earth!

Well, the herd came on, the bulls moaning and switching and cocking up their short, tufted tails, and presently the coulee was full of the animals as far as we could see. We had drawn back from the edge of the shelf and sat motionless, only our heads in view, and so we remained until the head of the long column had passed out into the bottom. I then leaned forward, and Red Crow sprang to his feet, and we began shooting down, choosing always animals with the broadest, most rounding hips, and therefore the fattest meat. With my rifle, and one after the other my pistols, I shot three good cows, and Red Crow shot four with his bow and arrows. All seven of them fell close around the mouth of the coulee. Those that had passed out into the bottom, unhurt, ran off down the valley. The rest, back up the coulee, turned and went up on the plain, in their hurry and scrambling raising such a cloud of dust that we nearly strangled in it. We got down from the shelf and began butchering our kills, taking only the best of the meat with the hides. We got into the camp before sundown, our horses staggering under their heavy loads. We had broiled tongue for our evening meal.

Yes, buffalo tongue, a whole one each of us, and some service berries, were what the women set before us that evening. How is it that I remember all those little details of the vanished years? I cannot remember what happened last year, or the year before, yet all of that long ago time is as plain to me as my hand before my face!

The next morning, with pieces of dry meat and back fat in our hands for breakfast, Red Crow and I rode out of camp at daylight for a day on the cliffs. On the previous day we had seen numbers of bighorn along them, and, opposite the mouth of the coulee where we had killed the buffaloes, had discovered what we thought was the entrance to a cave. We wanted to see that. We had told Mink Woman that she could not go with us, but after going down the valley for a mile or more found her close at our heels. Nor would she go back: "I want to see that cave as much as you do," she said. "I help you hunt, and butcher your kills; it is only fair that you do something for me now and then."

It was a beautiful morning, clear, cool, windless. As we rode along we saw deer and elk dodging out of our way, a beaver now and then and coveys of sage hens and prairie grouse. While waiting for the buffaloes to come in, the day before, we had looked out a way by which we thought it would be possible to reach the cave, and now, leaving the horses a half mile or more above our stand on the shelf, we began the ascent of the cliffs. The cave was located at the back of a very long shelf about two thirds of the way up the canyon side, and we believed that we could reach its western end by climbing the series of small shelves and sleep slopes under that part of it.

We climbed a fifty-foot slope of fallen boulders and came to the first shelf, a couple of feet higher than our heads, and Red Crow told me to use his back as a mount, and go up first. He leaned against the rock wall, bending over. I handed my gun to Mink Woman and, stepping up on his back and then on his shoulders, and steadying myself by keeping my hands against the wall, straightened up; and as my head rose above the level of the shelf I saw something that made me gasp.

CHAPTER VI
CAMPING ON ARROW RIVER

With flattened ears and a menacing snarl a mountain lion, not four feet back, was crouching and nervously shuffling her forefeet for a spring at me, and three or four small young ones behind her all had their backs arched and were spitting and growling too. I ducked down so quickly that I lost my balance and tumbled onto the rocks, but luckily the fall did not hurt me. I was up on my feet at once.

"What was it?" Red Crow asked.

"A big lion! It has little young ones. It was making ready to spring at me," I answered, and at that he became greatly excited.

"Quick! Let me have your gun! Help me up!" he exclaimed, and I went to the wall and bent over, and Mink Woman handed him the gun after he had gotten upon my back. He straightened up, and I expected to hear him shoot; but instead he called down to us: "They are gone!" and sprang upon the shelf and we heard a scuff or two of his moccasins as he ran off. At that Mink Woman helped me get upon the shelf, and I then drew her up, and we ran around a bend of it just in time to see Red Crow, farther on, lay down my gun, draw his bow and arrows, and begin shooting at something that seemed to be in a crevice of the cliff at the back of the shelf. We hurried on to him and found that he had killed the lion there where she had made her stand in front of her young, and as we came up to him he shot the last of the little ones. There were four of them. He was mightily pleased at what he had done, for the hide of a mountain lion was valued by the Blackfeet tribes above that of any other animal. It was believed to bring good luck in hunting and in war to the owner, and was either fashioned into a bow case and quiver, or softly tanned and used as a saddle robe.

While we were skinning the animals I asked my friend why he had not used my gun to kill the old one.

"Never the gun when the bow will do as well!" he answered. "The bow is silent. The gun goes whoom! and for far around all ears take notice of it."

There was sound sense in what he said. I determined that I would no longer delay getting a bow and learning to use it. We little thought that we were to prove his saying on the height above us. If he had fired the gun at the lion it is likely that I would not be sitting here telling you my story of those vanished days.

Having skinned the lions we folded the hides flesh side together, so that they would not dry out, and would be fresh and soft to stretch properly when we got them to camp, and packed them with us; they were light and would not interfere with our climbing. We went back to where we had come up on the shelf, and then zigzagged our way up from shelf to shelf, all the time in a deep recess in the great cliff. On the shelf above the one on which we got the lions, were the remains of a yearling bighorn which the old lion had apparently killed that morning, and that explained, we thought, why we had seen none of the animals thereabout. On the previous day we had seen several small bands there.

At last we climbed onto the cave shelf. From where we struck it, it ran out toward the valley and then circled around the projecting point of the formation, and ended in a recess similar to the one we had come up in. The cave was on our side of the point; about a hundred yards from it. We hurried out along the shelf, eager to get to the cave and explore it, but upon reaching the entrance our haste died right there; it was a mighty black hole we were looking into; a rank, damp, cold odor came from it; we could see in only a few yards; the darkness beyond might conceal something of great danger to us! A grizzly, I thought, and my companions' fears included ghosts; the shadows of the dead always lurking about to do the living harm.

Said Red Crow at last, and the set expression of his face belied his words: "Ha! I am not afraid! Let's go in!"

"Come on," I told him, and led the way.

"I am afraid! I shall wait for you here!" Mink Woman told us. But she didn't. We had taken but a few steps when she was close behind us, feeling safest there.

A few yards in, the cave narrowed to but little more than three feet, and then widened out again into a big, jagged-walled and high-roofed room. We could see but little of it at first, for we were blocking the light; but after leaving the narrow passage, and as our eyes became accustomed to the darkness, we saw that the room was the end of the cave. We stood still, hardly breathing, listening for any movement there; watching for shining eyes; and at last concluded that the place was harmless enough. Then I, farthest in, saw something, a dim, white, queerly shaped object on the floor at the back of the room. I stared at it a long time, made sure that whatever it was it had no life, and then moved on. The others then saw it and Red Crow exclaimed: "What is it? What is it?"

We moved on again, and saw at last that our find was a number of painted and fringed rawhide war cylinders, receptacles in which warriors carried their war bonnets and war clothes when on a raid.

"Ghosts' property! Do not touch them!" Mink Woman exclaimed, but I was already lifting one of them, and as I did so it gave off a fresh odor of sweet grass smoke, a medicine—a sacred perfume of the Blackfeet tribes, I knew. I held it under Red Crow's nose and he sniffed at it and exclaimed: "Newly smoked!" He then took it and held it up in better light, and pointed to the painted design: "Crow! Crow painting!" he exclaimed, and turned quickly and stared out the way we had come; so did I. There was no one in sight. All was quiet; but we felt sure that the enemy was not far away!

I turned back and counted the cylinders; there were seven, and with them were coils of rawhide rope, several bridles with Spanish bits, the first that I had ever seen, and didn't then know were of that make, and three square-shaped rawhide pouches with slings for carrying. I put my hand into one of them and brought forth a piece of freshly roasted meat! That settled it; a Crow war party was somewhere on the cliffs about us; they had perhaps slept here, and were now out on watch. I thought it strange that they had not seen us. Said Red Crow: "They must be sitting out around the point. Just think! If I had fired the gun at the lion we would now be without scalps!"

And at that he gave a little laugh; a scared little laugh, his eyes all the time on the cave entrance, as were mine, and Mink Woman's.

"What shall we do?" she whispered.

"Take these things and run," I said.

"No!" said Red Crow, and took from me the pouch, put the roast meat back and laid it in its place in the pile. "Come!" he said, and we followed him out. At the entrance we looked off along the length of the shelf as far as we could see its rounding curve; no one was in sight. We ran, ran for our lives back the way we had come, our backs twitching in expectation of arrow piercings. We reached the end of the shelf in the recess, halted a moment for a last look back, and seeing no one, went quickly down the slopes and over the shelves to the bottom, and thence to our picketed horses. Not until we reached them did we feel really safe.

"There! We survive!" Red Crow exclaimed. "I go for help! We shall wipe out those Crows! Hasten, you two; go down to the place of our buffalo killing and keep watch for them, but don't let them think that you know they are there on the cliffs. I shall come back as soon as I can."

He left us, and Mink Woman and I rode down to the mouth of the deep coulee, picketed our horses just below it, and then got onto the shelf from which we had shot the buffaloes the day before; and not until then did we actually begin our watch. I sat facing the bottom of the coulee, looking up it the most of the time just as though I were waiting for a herd of buffaloes to come down for water, and Mink Woman pretended to be looking up and down the canyon, but most of the time her eyes were upon the high, rounding point of the cliff opposite us, and in particular the cave shelf. We felt sure that somewhere up there the enemy lay concealed and was watching us. It was likely that, coming across the plain in the early morning, they had seen some of our people riding out to hunt, and had taken refuge in the cliff with the expectation of finding our camp and raiding our horses when night came.

It was mid-afternoon when we saw a number of riders, twenty or thirty, coming down the valley. They appeared to be in no haste, but when they had come close the sweat on their horses told us that they had ridden hard the most of the way down. Lone Walker was the leader of the party. He rode up close to our shelf and asked if we had seen the enemy while sitting there, and upon learning that we hadn't, said that Red Crow was guiding a big party to attack the Crows from the top of the cliff. He then turned to his men and told one of them to ride up the coulee, and the rest to watch him, in order that the Crows might not have the least suspicion that we were aware of their presence.

It was hard for us all to do that, to stare up a coulee when we wanted to keep our eyes on the cliffs, but we had not to endure it long; we soon heard the whoom! whoom! whoom! of guns, and turning, saw our men on the top of the rounding point of the cliff, and shooting down at three men running along the shelf on which was the entrance to the cave. They disappeared around the bend and I knew that they were making for shelter there. But whoom! whoom! went two guns back in the recess, and soon one of the men came running back. In the meantime some of our party had found a way down to the other end of the shelf, and now came running along it out around the point. As soon as the lone enemysaw them he stopped short, fired an arrow at them that went wild, and then with a quick leap threw himself from the shelf. Down, down he went, a sickening sight as he whirled through the air, and struck the rocks far below.

"Hai! Hai! Hai! A brave end!" cried Lone Walker, and all the party echoed his words, and several made a dash across to secure his scalp and weapons. Meantime one of our men up on the extreme point of the cliff was signaling down to us, his signs plain as he stood outlined against the clear sky: "They are all wiped out! Dead! We meet you at camp!" And at that we all got upon our horses and rode home.

The cliff party, bearing the scalps and plunder they had taken from the enemy, arrived in camp at the same time we did and were hailed with great acclaim. As soon as the greeting was over Red Crow handed me one of the fringed and painted cylinders that we had discovered in the cave. "Take it," he said, "it is yours. See, I also have one. We got them all."

We went to our lodge then with Lone Walker, and Red Crow told us how he had guided the big party out, stationing a few men down at the cave, in the first place, and then leading the others out upon the point above the shelf where he thought the enemy would be sitting. Upon looking over the edge they had found the seven Crows lying flat on the rocky projection straight below, all intently watching our party across at the mouth of the coulee. Four of them had been killed where they lay. Two of the three that then ran for the cave had been shot down before they could reach it. The last man, rather than give the Pi-kun-i the honor of killing him, had committed suicide by jumping from the cliff. "He was a coward! Had I been in his place I would have fought to the last; I would have tried my best to make others die with me!" Red Crow concluded.

"I like to hear you say that. Fight to the last! That is the one thing to do!" Lone Walker told him.

With no little eagerness Red Crow and I unlaced the round end covers of our Crow war cylinders, and drew out the contents, and found that we each had a beautiful war suit and eagle tail feather war bonnet. The streaming ends of the bonnets were feathered all the way, and were so long that they would drag at our heels as we walked. Then and there a visitor in the lodge offered me five horses for my costume. I would not have parted with it for any number of horses; I had nine head, all that I could possibly use while on the trail.

We camped on Arrow River all of a week, the women busily gathering choke-cherries for winter use. Upon bringing them into camp they pounded them, pits and all, on flat rocks, and set the mass on clean rawhides to dry, and then stored it in rawhide pouches. There was never enough of it for daily use. In its raw state, or stewed, or mixed with finely pounded dry meat and marrow grease—pemmican—it was passed around as a side dish to a feast. I liked it, and always ate my share, although never without some misgivings as to the effect of the sharp and indigestible particles of pounded pits in my stomach.

During our stay at this place an old, old man named Kip-i-tai-su-yi-kak-i (Old-Woman-Stretching-Her-Legs) came into our lodge one night, took his bow and quiver case from his back, passed it to me and said: "There, my son Rising Wolf! I heard that you wanted bow and arrows, so I give you this set, one that I took long ago in battle with the Snake People. It is a good bow. The arrows are well feathered and fly straight. I hope that you will have good success with my present, and sometimes remember that I am fond of broiled tongue!"

And at that he laughed, and we all laughed with him, and I said that he should not lack for tongues, and kept my word. I was very glad to get the bow. At first it was a little too stiff for the strength of my arms, but with daily use of it my muscles grew up to its requirement of strength, and I soon became a fair shot with the feathered shafts. I did not carry the bow all the time, but always used it for running buffaloes. On my first chase with it I killed three cows, and once, several years later, shot down thirteen cows with it in one run. But that was nothing. I once saw a man, named Little Otter, shoot twenty-seven buffaloes in one run! He was a big, powerfully built man, he rode a big, swift, well-trained, buffalo horse, and every time he let an arrow fly it slipped into an animal just back of the ribs and ranged forward into the heart and lungs.

You ask how a man happened to be named Old-Woman-Stretching-Her-Legs. When a child was born, a medicine man was called in to name it, and invariably the name he gave was of something he had seen, or of some incident, in one of his dreams, or, as he believed them to be, visions. Thus, in a dream, the medicine man had seen an old woman at rest, or sleeping, and she had stretched down her legs to get more ease. Hence the name. A woman generally retained through life the name given her at birth. A man, as I have explained, was entitled to take a new name every time he counted a big coup. Some odd names that I remember are Chewing-Black-Bones; Back-Coming-in-Sight; Tail-Feathers-Coming-in-Sight-over-the-Hill; Falling Bear; and He-Talked-with-the-Buffalo.

During the time of our encampment on Arrow River, Red Crow and I killed a number of fine bighorn rams along the cliffs, and the skins of these, tanned into soft leather and smoked by the women, were made into a shirt and leggings for me. It was time that I had them, for my one suit of company clothes was falling to pieces. Also, my shoes had given out. Attired now in leather clothes, breechclout, moccasins, and with a toga, or wrap of buffalo cow leather, I was all Indian except in color. Lone Walker himself made the suit for me. Men were their own tailors; the women made only their moccasins. In time I learned to cut out and sew my clothing.

Red Crow had become the owner of one of the two huge Spanish bits that we had found in the cave with the rest of the Crow belongings. It was beautifully fashioned of hand-forged steel, its long shanks inlaid with silver, and he took good care of it, polishing and cleaning it frequently. As he was thus occupied one evening, Lone Walker pointed to the bit and asked me if I knew whence it had come. I didn't, of course, and said so, whereupon he told Mink Woman to take down a long, well-wrapped roll of buckskin that was invariably fastened to the lodge poles above his couch. I had often wondered what it might contain. He undid the fastenings, unrolled wrap after wrap of leather, and held up to my astonished gaze a shirt of mail, very fine meshed and light, and an exquisitely fashioned rapier. He passed them to me for examination, and I found etched on the rapier blade the legend: "Francisco Alvarez. Barcelona. 1693." It was an old Spanish blade.

"The people who made the bit," he told me in signs and words, very slowly and carefully so that I would understand, "made these. They live in the Far Southland; the always-summer land. I went there once with a party of our people, traveling ever south all summer. We started from our country when the grass first started in the spring, and, counting the moons, arrived in that far Southland in the first moon of winter here. We found there white men different from those who had come to the Assiniboine River and built a fort. They were dark-skinned and black-haired, most of them. They had many horses. We went south to take their horses, and captured many of them. But not without a fight, several fights. In one of the fights I killed the man who wore this iron shirt and carried this big knife. We did not get back to our country until the middle of the next summer. That is a strong shirt. Arrows cannot pierce it. It has saved my life three different times in battle with the enemy."

Well, that was news to me, that these people went so very far, all the way to Mexico, on their raids. Afterward I heard many interesting tales of raids into the Far South, many parties going there in my time, and generally returning with great bands of horses and plunder taken from the Spanish, and from different Indian tribes. I learned that the Crows had the first horses that the Blackfeet tribes ever saw, and that they were almost paralyzed with astonishment when they saw men mount the strange, big animals and guide them in whatever direction they wished to go. But fear soon gave place to burning desire to own the useful animals, and they began raiding the herds of the Crows, the Snakes, and other Southern tribes, and the Spanish, and in time became owners of thousands of them through capture, and by natural increase. Lone Walker told me that his people first obtained horses when his father's father was a small boy, and as near as I could figure it, that was about 1680 to 1700. The acquisition of the horse caused a vast change in the life of the Blackfeet tribes. Before that time, with only their wolf-like dogs for beasts of burden, their wanderings had been limited to the forests of the Slave Lakes region, and the edge of the plains of the Saskatchewan. With horses for riding and packing, and, later, a few guns obtained from the Sieur de la Vérendrie's company, they swept southward and conquered a vast domain and became the terror of all surrounding tribes. The Blackfeet named the horse, po-no-ka-mi-ta (elk-dog), because, like the dog, it carried burdens, and was of large size, like the elk.

One evening, there at Arrow River, Lone Walker told me that we would ride out early the next morning, and he would show me a "white men's leavings,"—nap-i-kwaks o-kit-stuks-in, in his language. I asked him what it was, and was told to be patient; that I should see it. Accordingly, we rode out on the plain on the trail by which we had come down to the river, then turned sharply to the right, following the general course of the big, walled valley, and after several hours' travel came to a pile of rocks set on top of a low ridge on the plain, and at the head of a very long coulee, heading there and running down to the river, several miles away. "There! That is white men's leavings!" the chief exclaimed. "We know not how long ago they piled those rocks. It was in my father's time that our people found the pile, just as you see it, except that at that time a white metal figure of a man against black, crossed sticks, his arms outstretched, was stuck in the top of it, so that it faced yonder Belt Mountains."

I was tremendously interested. "What became of the man figure?" I asked.

"The finder kept it for some time, and then sacrificed it to the sun; hung it to the roof of a medicine lodge," he answered, and it seemed strange to think that an image of Jesus had been presented to a pagan god.

"How long ago do you think it was that white men put up this pile?" I asked.

"Fifty, maybe sixty, maybe seventy winters. In my father's time white men came to the camp of the Earth House People. It was in winter time. They rode horses; wore iron shirts; carried guns with big, flaring muzzles, and long knives. From the camp of the Earth House People they went west, returned soon, and went back north, whence they had come. None of our tribes saw them."

I said to myself: "The Sieur de la Vérendrie's party must have put up this monument, and yonder Belt Mountains must be those that they named the Shining Mountains!"

Well I knew the story of the brave and unfortunate Sieur. My grandfather, who had had some interest in his ventures, had related it many times. Because of enemies who had the favor of the Court, in France, he had failed in his undertakings to establish a great fur trade in the West, and he had died of a broken heart! I must confess that I felt some disappointment upon learning that I was not, as I had thought, the first of my race to see this part of the country. However, the knowledge that I had been the first white person to traverse the great Saskatchewan-Missouri River country comforted me.

As we rode homeward I learned from Lone Walker that a man named Sees Far had discovered the monument and taken the cross. He was long since dead. I was afraid to ask where the medicine lodge was built at which the cross had been sacrificed to the sun. The penalty for robbing the sun was death. The Blackfeet tribes had too much reverence for their gods to do that, and war parties of other tribes, traveling through the country and coming upon a deserted medicine lodge, gave it a wide berth; they feared the power of the shining god for whom it had been built. I remember that the Kai-na tribe of the Blackfeet once came upon three free trappers (or were they the American Company's *engagés*—I forget) robbing a medicine lodge, and killed them all!

I come now to a part of my story that is not so very happy. On the morning that we broke the Arrow River camp, the chiefs, and the guard that generally rode ahead of the column, remained on the camp ground, gathered here and there in little groups smoking and telling stories, until long after the people had packed up and were traveling up the long coulee through which the trail led to the plain on the south side of the valley. I went on with Red Crow and Mink Woman, and a young man named Eagle Plume, Lone Walker's nephew, helping them herd along the chief's big band of horses in which, of course, were those that he had given me. As soon as we got out of the narrow confine of the coulee we drove the herd at one side of the beaten travois and pack trail, keeping about even with Lone Walker's outfit of women and children riders, and their loaded horses. Their place was at the head of the Little Robes Band, and that had its place in the long line about a half mile from the lead band, which was that of the Lone Eaters.

We had traveled three or four miles from the river, and were wending our way among a wide, long setting of rough hills, keeping ever in the low places between them, when, without the slightest warning, a large body of riders dashed out from behind a steep hill and made for the head of our column. Far off as they were, we could hear them raise their war song, and could see that they were all decked out in their war finery.

"Crows! Crows! They attack us!" I heard men crying as they urged their horses forward.

"Crows! We must help fight them!" Red Crow called to me, and like one in a dream I found myself with my companions riding madly for the front.

CHAPTER VII
THE CROWS ATTACK THE BLACKFEET

All the men from the whole length of the line were rushing forward, even the old and weak who had scarce strength enough to string their bows. Ahead, women and children were coming back as fast as they could make their horses run, and pack horses, travois horses, and those dragging lodge poles were running in all directions and scattering their loads upon the plain. It was a scene of awful confusion and of noise; women and children yelling and crying with fright, flying past us wild eyed, our men shouting to one another to hurry, to take courage, and above all, louder than all, the yells and shouts of the enemy and our few warriors there at the front.

The Crows were forcing our men back; they were fighting their best but were far outnumbered and, as we could see, were falling not a few. I looked back, and the sight of hundreds of our men coming on was encouraging. With my companions, and twenty or thirty more riders, I was now getting close to the fighting. The Crows, in one big, long body, were riding full speed across the stand our men were making, shooting their arrows and few guns as they passed, and wheeling out and around for another charge by them. This they had done many times, and so far as I could see, but few of them had fallen.

At last we were at the front, arriving there just as the Crows were making another of their wheeling charges. They must have been all of four hundred men, and we there facing them were not two hundred. On they came, to pass close on our right, shouting their war cry, their long-tailed war bonnets, the fringe of their beautiful clothes, the plumes of their shields all a-flutter in the wind. A brave sight they were, and fearsome! As they swept past us they shot their arrows, the air was full of them, and we shot at them. Several men on both sides went down, horses were wounded and became unmanageable in their fright, carrying their riders whither they willed. My horse was dancing with excitement and jerking on his bit, making it impossible for me to take steady aim, so I fired my gun at the thickest group of the passing riders and so far as I could see did them no harm.

AS THEY SWEPT PAST US THEY SHOT THEIR ARROWS

This time, instead of wheeling out and around for another charge, the Crow chief led his men straight on along the line of the fleeing women and children. Swarms of our men were coming out, and he no doubt concluded to do all the damage that he could before he would have to give way before our superior numbers. Upon seeing his intent, we, too, turned back, the men crying out to one another: "The women! The children! Fight hard for them!"

Out where the Crows had first struck our column there were dead and dying and wounded women and children, as well as men, and now more began to fall. The Crows were without mercy. Here were the people who had despoiled them; taken from them their vast hunting-ground; and now they should pay for it with their blood! They were so drunk with hatred that they were for the time reckless of harm to themselves.

We followed them close. Beyond, a great crowd of our men were riding at them, led by Lone Walker himself. I did not see what he did, I had eyes only for what was immediately around me, but I heard the tale of it many times afterward. He made straight for the Crow chief, and the latter for him, and they brought their horses together with such a shock that both fell. As they went down both men sprang free and grappled one another, Lone Walker dropping his empty gun, and the Crow letting go his bow and handful of arrows. A crowd surrounded them, the Crows endeavoring to aid their chief, our men fighting them off. The Crow chief had managed to get out his knife, but Lone Walker gave his arm such a sudden fierce twist that he dropped it, endeavored to recover it, and as he did so Lone Walker got out his own knife and stabbed him down through his back into his heart, and he fell and died!

In the meantime we were in a terrible scrimmage; a thick mixup of riders. I had stuck my gun in under my belt, there was no time to reload it, and had fired one of my pistols, and now got out the other one. Red Crow and I were side by side. He had shot away his handful of arrows and was reaching into his quiver for more when a Crow rode up beside him, reached out and grasped him by the arm, endeavoring to pull him over and knife him. I saw him just in time to poke my pistol over past Red Crow and fire, and down he went from his horse! The sight of him falling, his awful stare of hate—would you believe it, made me sick and sorry for him, enemy though he was! "I have killed a man! I have killed a man!" I said to myself as I replaced the pistol and got out my gun to use as a club, as I saw others doing. But just then I saw a wounded woman stagger to her feet, and then with a cry throw up her hands and fall dead, and I shouted with joy that I had killed, and with Red Crow dashed on, thirsting now to kill! kill! kill! Right there, and for all time vanished my doubts, my tender-heartedness! The enemies of the Pi-kun-i were my enemies so long as they tried to do me harm!

Their chief dead, and faced by ever-increasing numbers of our warriors, the Crows now turned and fled, but we did not chase them far; our men were so anxious about their families, to learn if they were safe, or dead, that they had no heart for the pursuit. It was a terrible sight that met our eyes as we turned and went back to that part of the trail that had been the scene of the fight; everywhere along it were dead and wounded men and women and children and horses. I could not bear to look at them, and was glad when Lone Walker told a number of us to round up the pack and travois horses scattered out upon the plain, and drive them back to the river, where we would go into camp and bury the dead. We were a long time doing that, necessarily leaving the packs that had fallen for the owners to recover later. When we got back to the river with our drive we found many lodges already up, including our two. None of Lone Walker's great family had been harmed, nor had they met any loss of property. Red Crow and I got a hasty bite to eat, and catching fresh horses went with a strong guard that was to remain out on the plain until all the dead had been carried in for burial, and all the scattered property recovered. That was all done before sunset, and then a guard was placed about camp for the night, and another told off to herd the horses.

That was a sad evening. Everywhere in camp there was wailing for the dead; everywhere medicine men were praying for the wounded, chanting their sacred songs as they went through strange ceremonies for curing them. The chiefs gathered in our lodge to bitterly blame themselves for not having been out at the front, with the guard ahead of them, when camp was broken. They had taken count of our loss: forty-one men, thirty-two women and girls, and nine children were dead and buried—the trees in the near grove were full of them—and some of the wounded were sure to die. The Crows had lost sixty-one of their number, and some of their wounded would undoubtedly die. Not then, nor for many a night afterward, did anyone tell what he had particularly done in the fight against the enemy. It was surmised that, in wiping out the seven Crows on the cliff, another member of the party, perhaps on watch elsewhere, had been overlooked; and that he had gone home and brought his people to attack us. There were two tribes of the enemy: the River Crows and the Mountain Crows. If camping together, they were too strong for the Pi-kun-i to attack. That very evening three messengers were selected to go north to the Kai-na, camping somewhere in the Bear Paw Mountains, and ask them to come down and join in a raid against the enemy.

I pass over the ensuing days of sadness, in which seven of the wounded died. As soon as the others were well enough to travel we moved on, camped one night on O-to-kwi-tuk-tai, Yellow River, or as Lewis and Clark named it, Judith River, and the next day moved east to a small stream named It-tsis-ki-os-op (It-Crushed-Them). Years later it was named Armell's Creek after an American Fur Company man who built a trading post at its junction with the Missouri. The Blackfoot name was given it for the reason that some women, when digging red paint in the foot of a high cutbank bordering the stream, had been killed by a heavy fall of the earth.

The stream rises in the midst of some high, flat-topped buttes crowned with a sparse growth of scrub pine and juniper, and its valley is well timbered with pine and cottonwood. Its head is only a few miles from the foot of the Mut-si-kin-is-tuk-ists (Moccasin Mountains). On the morning after we went into camp I rode out to hunt with Red Crow, and he took me to the extreme head of the stream, which was a large spring under an overhang of wall rock. This sloped up from the sands of the floor on the right of the spring to a height of six or seven feet on the outside of the spring, and was of dark brown volcanic rock. Originally very rough, as the extreme outer and inner portion attested, this roof had in the course of ages been rubbed smooth by the animals that had come there to drink at the spring. All that had come, from small antelopes to huge buffaloes, had found the right height of it against which to rub their backs, and they had rubbed and rubbed until the whole roof as high as they could touch it was as smooth and lustrous as glass. I could see my face in it.

While standing there we heard some animals coming along one of the many trails in the surrounding timber, and presently saw that they were a file of bull elk. We had left our horses some distance back, so they saw nothing to alarm them. When they were within thirty feet of us Red Crow let fly an arrow at the leader, and the others stopped and stared at him as he fell, and struggled fruitlessly to regain his feet. That gave my companion time to slip an arrow into another one, and then I fired and dropped a third, and we had all the meat that we wanted. We butchered the three, and then went home and sent Lone Walker's nephew and some of the women out with pack horses for the meat.

From the time that the Crows made their terrible attack upon us, we kept a strong guard with the horses night and day, and kept scouting parties far out on the plains watching for the possible return of the enemy. Some men who had been sent to trail the Crows to their camp, returned in eight or nine days' time and reported that it was on The-Other-Side Bear River (O-pum-ohst Kyai-is-i-sak-ta), straight south from the pass in the Moccasin Mountains. This is the Musselshell River of Lewis and Clark. The Blackfoot name for it distinguishes it from their other Bear River, the Marias.

The returning scouts said that the camp was very large, and in two parts, showing that both tribes of the Crows were there. Said Lone Walker when he got the news: "And so they have dared to come back into our land and hunt our game! Ha! As soon as the Kai-na come we shall make them pay dearly for that!"

The talk now was all of war. In every tree about the camp were hung the warriors' offerings to the sun, placed there with prayers to the god to give them success in the coming battle.

As I have said, the camp was always pitched in a big circle of the clan groups. Inside this circle were nine lodges set in a smaller circle, each one painted with a sacred, or "medicine" design, no two of them alike. The one always set nearest to our Small Robes group of lodges was owned by a great warrior named Mi-nik-sa-pwo-pi (Mad Plume), and had for its design a huge buffalo bull and a buffalo cow in black, the heart, and the life line running to it from the mouth, painted bright red. I had not thought that these lodges had any especial significance, but I was soon to know better. On the day after we killed the elk at the shining rock spring, Red Crow pointed to the buffalo medicine lodge and said to me: "Just think; we are invited there to-night! We are asked to join the Braves!"

"He does not understand," said Lone Walker, standing near us. "Let us sit here, White Son, and I will explain."

We sat there in front of our lodge, and the chief began: "Those nine are the lodges of the chiefs of the All Friends Society. It has nine different bands: the Braves, All-Crazy-Dogs, Raven Carriers, Dogs, Tails, Horns, Kit-Foxes, Siezers, and Bulls. To become a member of one of the bands one has to be of good heart, of a straight tongue, generous, and of proved bravery; so you see that you are thought to be all that, else you would not be asked to join this band of Braves, made up of our young warriors. I am a member of the Bulls, our oldest warriors. All the bands are under the orders of myself and my brother clan chiefs. There! Now you understand!"

But I didn't. I learned in time, however, that this great I-kun-uh-kat-si, or All Friends Society, had for its main object the carrying out—under the direction of the chiefs—of the tribal laws. If a man or woman was to be punished, it was a band of the society that meted it out, after the chiefs decided what the punishment should be. In battle the members of a band hung close together, shouting the name of it, and encouraging one another to do their best. Each band had its particular songs, and its own peculiar way of dancing. Its chief's lodge was its headquarters, and there of an evening the members were wont to gather for a social time, for a little feast, singing, and story telling as the pipe went round the circle.

When Red Crow and I went into the Braves' lodge that evening, Mad Plume made us welcome, and indicated that we should sit at his left. That was the only space left; all the rest was occupied by his family, and members of the band, who also gave us pleasant greeting.

"Now, then, young men," Mad Plume said to us as soon as we were seated, "we have had our eyes upon you for some time, thinking to invite you to join us. We learned that you are good-hearted, generous, truthful, that you are good to the old. We but waited to learn what you would do before the enemy, and we learned; the other day when the Crows attacked us you each did your best; you each did your share in driving them off, and each killed. So now we ask: Would you like to become Braves?"

"Yes! Yes!" we exclaimed.

"And will you always obey the orders of the tribes' chiefs, and the Braves' chief?"

"Yes! Yes!"

"Then you are Braves!" he concluded. And all present signified their approval. I can't begin to tell you how pleased I was, how proud of this unexpected honor. And at last I felt absolutely safe with the Pi-kun-i; felt that they considered me one of them in every respect.

There were countless herds of game in all directions from our camp there on It-Crushed-Them. By day the hunters scattered it, but it was the mating season of the buffaloes, they were very uneasy, constantly on the move, and fresh herds took the place of those that were frightened away. One day when Red Crow and I were out after meat, with Mink Woman trailing us with a couple of pack horses, we saw a small band of buffaloes lying on a side hill, and leaving our horses in the shelter of the timber around the shining rock spring, approached them. We followed up a shallow coulee that headed close to the resting animals, in places crawling upon hands and knees in order to keep under the shelter of low banks. Mink Woman followed us close. We had asked her to remain with the horses, but she was determined to be right with us and see the shooting at close range.

We were still several hundred yards from the buffaloes, much too far for Red Crow's arrows, and even my gun, when we heard the moaning bellow of bulls off to our left. We paid no attention to it; there had been no buffaloes in sight in that direction, and we thought that the animals making it were a long way off. That deep, muffled bellowing, however, was wonderfully deceiving; just by the sound of it, without looking, one could never determine if the animals making it were near by, or a mile or so away. But now we were suddenly warned that the bulls we heard were close; we could hear the rushing thud of their feet, and two appeared just a few yards ahead of us, attacking one another on the edge of the coulee and slipping sideways down the steep bank, head pressed against head.

"They are mad! Don't shoot, don't move, else they may attack us!" Red Crow told me, and Mink Woman, just back of us, heard him.

But they were not all; only two of a band of thirty or forty, all bulls, all outcasts from different herds, mad at one another and at all the world. The two fighting incited others to fight, and the rest, moaning and tossing their heads, switching their short tails, were soon all around us. They presented a most frightful spectacle! Their dark eyes seemed to shoot fire from under the overhanging shaggy hair; several more engaged in fights, and some of those afraid to do that attacked the bank of the coulee and with their sharp horns gouged out pieces of turf and tossed them in every direction. We dared not move; we hardly dared breathe; our suspense was almost unbearable. Said Mink Woman at last: "Brother, I am terribly frightened. I think that I shall have to run!"

"Don't you do it! No running unless we are about to be stepped upon!" he answered. An old bull standing not twenty feet from us heard the low talk, whirled around and stared at us. Anyhow I thought that it was at us, but if it was, he likely did not distinguish us from the rocks and sage brush among which we were lying. If he charged us I intended to shoot him in the brain, and then we should have to take our chances running from the others. But just then a bellowing started off where the band was that we had been approaching, and he turned and went leaping out of the coulee toward it, others following, leaving but two sets fighting in front of us. At that Mink Woman, no longer able to stand the strain, sprang to her feet and ran down the coulee, we then following her and looking back to see if we were pursued. The fighters paid no attention to us, but we kept running and never stopped until we reached our horses. Then, looking up the hill, we saw that the bulls had mingled with the band that we had been after, and all were traveling off to the south.

"Hai! We have had a narrow escape!" Red Crow exclaimed, and went on to tell me that outcast bulls were very dangerous. The hunters never tried to approach them on foot, and generally kept well away from them even when well mounted. Mink Woman listened, still shaking a little from the fright she had had, and then told me that only the summer before a mad bull had attacked a woman near camp and pierced her through the back with one of his horns, upon which she hung suspended despite his efforts to shake her off. Becoming frightened then, and blinded by her wrap, he had rushed right into camp and into a lodge, upsetting it and trampling its contents until killed by the men. He fell with the woman still impaled upon his horn. She was dead!

As we mounted and rode on, Red Crow told other instances of people being killed by outcast bulls. He said that bulls with a herd were not bad; that the cows would always run from the hunter, and they with them. We proved that in less than an hour, for we again approached the band that had been on the hillside, the outcast bulls now with it, and in a short run killed three cows, the bulls sprinting their best to outrun our horses.

Except for playing children and quarreling dogs, ours was a very quiet camp those days there on It-Crushed-Them. The people still mourned for their dead and, for that matter, did so for a year or more. Those not mourning had no heart for social pleasure. All waited impatiently for the coming of the Kai-na. Day after day the medicine men got out their sacred pipes and smoked and prayed to the gods to give the warriors great success against the Crows, still encamped upon The-Other-Side Bear River, as the scouts kept reporting. I wondered if the Crows had scouts out keeping equally close watch upon our camp.

One morning Lone Walker sent Red Crow and me to the Black Butte, the extreme eastern end of the Moccasin Mountains, with dried meat and back fat for the four scouts stationed there. We started very early, arrived at the foot of the butte by something like ten o'clock, and there left our horses in a grove of cottonwoods, and began the ascent with our packs of meat. It was a long, steep, winding climb up around to its southern slope, and thence to its summit, and we did not attain it until mid-afternoon. We found two of the watchers asleep in a little enclosure of rocks just under the summit, and the two others sitting upon the highest point. They had seen us approaching the butte on our horses, and were expecting us. They had no word for us to take back; no enemies had appeared, the country seemed to be free from them.

It was from this high point that I got my first good view of the Bear Paw, and Wolf Mountains, across on the north side of the Missouri, and the great plains of the Missouri-Musselshell country. The plains were black with buffaloes as far out in all directions as the eye could distinguish them. I cannot begin to tell you how glad I was to be there on that high point looking out upon that vast buffalo plain, its grand mountains, its sentinel buttes, and deep-gashed river valleys. I had a sense of ownership in it all. White though my skin, and blue my eyes, I was a member of a Blackfoot tribe, yes, even a member of its law and order society. And so, in common with my red people, an owner of this great hunting-ground!

And even as I was thinking that, Red Crow turned from a long lookout upon it and said to me: "Rising Wolf, brother, what a rich, what a beautiful land is ours!"

No, that doesn't express it; he said, "Ki-sak-ow-an-on!" (Your land and ours!)

"Ai! That is truth!" I answered, and we hastened down the steep butte, mounted our horses and went homeward across the plain.

We arrived in camp to find the messengers returned from the north. With them had come several hundred warriors of the Kai-na, and the whole tribe would be with us on the following day. For the first time since the fight with the Crows our camp livened up; feasts were prepared in many lodges for our guests, and later in the evening several bands of the All Friends Society gave dances in which they joined. For the first time, I put on my Crow war suit and joined in the dance of the Braves. As I had been practicing the step all by myself in the brush, I did quite well, and even got some praise.

The Kai-na trailed in and set up their lodges just below us the next afternoon. I counted the lodges and found that there were eleven hundred and thirty, including twenty-five or thirty lodges of Gros Ventres. All together we were a camp of nearly three thousand lodges—about fifteen thousand people. I looked out at the horses grazing upon the plain; there was no estimating the number; there were thousands and thousands of them!

That evening Eagle Ribs, head chief of the Kai-na, came with his clan chiefs to our lodge to council with Lone Walker and his clan chiefs. They all used such big words to express what they had to say that I would never have known what the talk was about had they not also used signs, these for the benefit of the Gros Ventre clan chief, who did not understand the Blackfoot language anywhere near as well as I did. The council lasted far into the night. When it broke up the decision was that we were to break camp early in the morning, travel all day on the trail to the Crow camp, and on the following morning go on, the warriors as fast as possible, the rest at the usual pace. It was the general opinion that we could strike the Crow camp early in the afternoon of the second day.

CHAPTER VIII
IN THE YELLOW RIVER COUNTRY

On the following evening we camped upon a small stream flowing into the Musselshell through a wide valley lying between the Moccasin Mountains, and another outlying shoot from the Rockies, named Kwun-is-tuk-ists (Snow Mountains). Not so named because they were more snowy than other mountains, but for their white rock formation. From a distance large bare areas of this on the dark, timbered slopes have all the appearance of snow banks.

The two great camps of us were certainly lively enough that evening. In the early part of it there was much dancing and feasting, many gatherings in the lodges of the medicine men for prayers, and sacrifices for success on the morrow, and later on the men laid out their war suits and war bonnets ready to put on in the morning. A big fire was lighted soon after dark to call in the watchers from the high points along the Moccasins, and the Snow Mountains, all of them excepting those upon the trail in the gap of the latter, from which they kept watch upon the camp of the enemy.

Late in the evening, nearly midnight it was, one of these last came in and told Lone Walker that the Crows seemed to be unaware of our approach, and at sundown their camp must still have been in the river valley, for they had not been seen trailing out from there. During the day movements of the buffaloes had shown that their hunters had been out from both sides of the valley for meat.

On the following morning we were all up before daylight, eating hurried meals that the women set before us, looking over our weapons, and anxious to be on our way. And the women were just as anxious that we start, for they wanted to pack up and follow as fast as they could; they were expecting to become rich with Crow property that day. Soon after daylight we mounted our best horses and were off, the Pi-kun-i and Kai-na chiefs, and the Ut-se-na, or Gros Ventre, chief with them in the lead, we following, band after band of the All Friends Society. All the Blackfeet tribes had this Society.

At mid-forenoon, when we topped the pass in the Snow Mountains, we found there our watchers awaiting us with somewhat disturbing news; they had not that morning seen any movement of the Crows out on the plain from their camp. Other mornings they had appeared on the plains on both sides of the river, rounding up their horses, riding out to hunt.

"Maybe they have discovered what we are up to, and have struck out for their country off there across Elk River," Lone Walker said to Eagle Ribs.

"Ai! One of their war parties may have seen us. If they did, they had plenty of time to get in with the news; we did not travel fast," said the Kai-na chief.

"Well, let us hurry on!" Lone Walker cried, and away we went down the pass and out upon the plain.

"It is just as I thought," I said to myself. "If we could keep a watch upon their camp, they could upon ours. They saw the Kai-na joining us, and have fled!"

It was a long way from the foot of the mountains out across the plain to the river; all of twenty miles, I should say. We made the length of it at a killing pace, and when, at last, we arrived at the rim of the valley our horses were covered with sweat, gasping for breath and about done for. Here and there in the big, long bottom under us a number of scattered lodges and hundreds of standing pole sets, told of the hurried flight of the Crows. We went down to the camp and examined it, and learned by raking out the fireplaces that it had been abandoned the previous evening. In the hurry of their going, they had left about all of their heavy property, all of their lodge pole sets, many lodges complete, and no end of*parflèches* and pack pouches filled with dried meat and tongues, pemmican, and dried berries. There was also much other stuff scattered about: rolls of leather; tanned and partly tanned buffalo robes for winter use; moccasins, used, and new, and beautifully embroidered; and many pack saddles and ropes.

"Well, brothers, all this will make our women happy," said Eagle Ribs, with a wave of his hand around.

"Ai! Some of them. It will not lighten the hearts of those who mourn!" said Lone Walker.

"And we cannot now lighten them! The Crows have a night's start of us, and our horses are so tired that we cannot overtake them," said Mad Plume.

"Before night they will cross Elk River and fortify themselves so strongly in timber, or on hill, that it will be impossible for us to carry the position!" another exclaimed.

All the chiefs agreed to that, and then Lone Walker said: "All that we can do is to keep parties out after their horses as long as we re main in this south part of our country. That, and the great loss of their property here, will teach them to remain upon their own hunting-ground."

The whole party then dismounted, some gathering in groups for a smoke, others scattering out to wander in the deserted camp and gather up for their women whatever took their fancy. Red Crow and I rode to the upper camp and had great fun going from lodge to lodge and examining the heaps of stuff that the Crows had abandoned. My quest was for fur, and I collected nine beaver and two otter skins.

That evening the chiefs held another council. Some were for giving the Crows time to get over their scare, and then going down into their country— all the warriors of both our tribes, and taking them by surprise and wiping them out. Lone Walker said that to do that we would have to lose a great many men; that he thought his plan, to keep them poor in horses, was the best. Finally, I was asked to give my opinion on the matter. I had been thinking a lot about it, and in signs, and with what words I could command, spoke right out:

"When I saw the women killed by the Crows, I was so angry that I wanted to help you fight until all the Crows were dead, but I do not feel so now," I told them. "You have done great wrongs to the Crows; back there on Arrow River they did only what you have done to them. Here is a great, rich country, large enough for all. I would like to see you make peace with the Crows, they agreeing to remain on their side of Elk River, and you on your side of it."

"Ha! Your white son has a gentle heart!" a Kai-na chief told Lone Walker.

"If you mean that he has an afraid heart, you are mistaken. In the fight the other day, he killed an enemy who was about to kill my son, Red Crow," Lone Walker answered, and at that the chief clapped a hand to his mouth in surprise and approval, and his manner quickly changed to one of great friendliness to me.

Said Lone Walker to me then: "My son, what you propose cannot be done. We have twice made peace with the Crows, the last time right here on this river, and both times they broke it within a moon. It was five summers back that we made the last peace with them. It was agreed that we should remain on the north side of Elk River, they on the south side, and neither tribe should raid the other's horse herds. The two tribes of us camped here side by side for many days, making friends with one another. We gave feasts for the Crows, they gave feasts for us. Every day there was a big dance in their camp, or in ours. A young Crow and one of our girls fell in love with one another, and we let him have her. Well, at last we parted from the Crows and started north, and had gone no farther than Yellow River when one of their war parties, following us, fell upon some of our hunters and killed four, one escaping wounded. So you see how it is: the Crows will not keep their word; it is useless to make peace with them."

On the next evening a mixed party of our and Kai-na warriors, about a hundred men, set out on foot to raid the Crow horse herds. They were going to take no chances; their plan was to travel nights, to find the Crows and watch for an opportunity to run off a large number of their stock.

The two tribes of us were too many people to camp together, so many hunters scattering the game, so that after a few days we were obliged to go a long way from camp to get meat. Another council was held and the chiefs decided that we, the Pi-kun-i, should winter in the upper Yellow River country, and the Kai-na on the Missouri, between the mouth of Yellow River and the mouth of the stream upon which we were then camping. Two days later we broke camp and went our way.

We struck Yellow River higher up than where we had crossed it coming out, and went into camp in a big, timbered bottom through which flowed a small stream named Hot Spring Water. On the following day Red Crow took me to the head of it, only a few miles from its junction with Yellow River, and there I saw my first hot spring. It was very large, and deep, and the water so hot that I could not put my hand in it.

Our camp here was at the foot, and east end of the Yellow Mountains. In the gap between them and the Moccasin Mountains, rose the hot spring in a beautiful, well grassed valley. Never in all my wanderings have I seen quite so good a game country as that was, and for that matter continued to be for no less than sixty years from that time.

As soon as we went into camp the chiefs put the hunting law into effect: from that time no one was allowed to hunt buffaloes when and where he willed. A watch was kept upon the herds, and when one came close to camp the chiefs' crier went all among the lodges calling out that the herd was near, and that all who wished to join in the chase should catch up their runners and gather at a certain place. From there the hunters would go out under the lead of some chief, approach the herd under cover, and then dash into it and make a big run, generally killing a large number of the animals. The strict observance of this law meant plenty of buffalo meat for all the people all the time, secured close to camp instead of far out on the winter plains. There was no law regarding the hunting of the mountain game, the elk, deer, and bighorns. They were not killed in any great number, for they became poor in winter, whereas the buffaloes retained their thick layer of fat until spring. And buffalo meat was by far the best, the most nutritious, the most easily digested. One never tired of it, as he did of the meat of other game.

When the leaves began to fall the real work of the winter was started, the taking of beavers for trade at our Mountain Fort. The streams were alive with them, and so tame were they that numbers were killed with bow and arrow. I myself killed several in that way, lying in wait for them at dams they were building, or on their trails to their wood cutting and dragging operations. But when winter came, and the ponds and streams froze over and they retired to their snug houses in the ponds, and dens in the stream banks, the one way then to get them was by setting traps, through the ice, at the entrances to their homes; they came out daily to their sunken piles of food sticks, dragged back what they wanted and ate the bark, and then took the stripped sticks out into the water, where they drifted off with the current.

By the time real winter set in, about all the beavers for miles around had been caught, and then most of the trappers rested. Red Crow, however, was so anxious to obtain pelts enough for the purchase of one of our company guns that he would not stop, and finally persuaded his father to allow us to go over on the head of Arrow River and trap there for a time. Red Crow's mother, Sis-tsa-ki, wanted to go with us, but Lone Walker said that he couldn't possibly spare his sits-beside-him wife, but another one, named Ah-wun-a-ki (Rattle Woman), and Red Crow's sister, Mink Woman, were allowed to go along to look after our comfort. A small lodge, lining and all, was borrowed for our use, and we started out in fine shape, taking five pack and travois horses to carry our outfit, and each riding a good horse. We made Arrow River that day, and camped pretty well on the head of it before noon the next day.

"Now, then, mother, and brother, and sister," said Red Crow after we had unpacked the horses, "we shall eat only the very best food here, and to begin, we will have stuffed entrail for our evening meal. Put up the lodge, you two, and get plenty of wood for the night, and Rising Wolf and I will go kill a fat buffalo cow."

There were a number of small bands of buffaloes in the breaks of the valley, and approaching the nearest one of them, I shot a fine young cow. We butchered it, took what meat we wanted, and a certain entrail that was streaked its whole length with threads of soft, snow-white fat. When we got to camp with our load, Rattle Woman took this entrail from us, washed it thoroughly in the stream, and brought it back to the lodge. She then cut some loin meat, or, as the whites call it, porterhouse steak, into small pieces about as large as hazel nuts and stuffed the entrail with it, the entrail being turned inside out in the process. Both ends of the entrail were then tied fast with sinew thread, and she placed it on the coals to broil, frequently turning it to keep it from burning. It was broiled for about fifteen minutes, shrinking considerably in that time, and was then thrown into a kettle of water and boiled for about fifteen minutes, and then we each took a fourth of its length and had our feast. Those who have never had meat cooked in this manner know not what good meat is! The threads of white fat on the entrail, it was turned inside out, you remember, gave it the required richness, and the tying of the ends kept in all the rich juices of the meat, something that cannot be done by any other method of cooking. The Blackfoot name for this was is-sap-wot-sists (put-inside-entrail). Their name for the Crows was Sap-wo, an abbreviation of the word, and I have often wondered if they did not learn this method of meat cooking from them during some time of peace between the two tribes.

There were so many of us in Lone Walker's family that we never had enough is-sap-wot-sists, the highest achievement of the meat cooker's art. But here on Arrow River the four of us in our snug lodge, with game all about us, had it every day, with good portions of dried berries that we had taken from the abandoned Crow camp. We certainly lived high! Red Crow had four traps, I had five. We set them carefully in ponds and along the stream, and each morning made the round of them, skinned what beavers we caught, and took the hides to the woman and girl to flesh and stretch upon rude hoops to dry. We had success beyond my wildest dreams, our traps averaging six beavers a night. It was virgin ground; traps had never been set there, the beavers were very unsuspicious and tame, and very numerous. The days flew by; our eagerness for our work increased rather than diminished. I was to be no gainer by it in pounds, shillings, and pence; whatever fur I caught was the property of the Company, but that made no difference; my ambition was to become an expert trapper and plainsman, and in that way get a good standing with the Company.

At the end of a month there we had a visit from Lone Walker's nephew. The chief had become uneasy about us, and had sent him to tell us to return. We were doing too well to go back then, and answered that we would trail in before the end of another month. We were really in no danger; the weather was cold, except for an occasional Chinook wind, there was considerable snow on the ground, and even in mild winters war parties were seldom abroad. So we trapped on and on, killed what meat we wanted, —oh, it was a happy time to me. Nor were our evenings around the lodge fire the least of it. My companions night after night told stories of the gods; stories of the adventures and the bravery of heroic Blackfeet men and women, all very interesting and instructive to me. At last came a second summons from Lone Walker for us to return, and this time we heeded it; we had anyhow pretty well cleaned out the beavers, getting only one or two a night for some time back. But Red Crow had to go in for more horses before we could move, the horses we had with us not being enough to pack our catch, and the lodge and other things. We took in with us, in ten skin bales, two hundred and forty beaver skins and nine otter skins, of which a few more than half were mine! Our big catch was the talk of the camp for several days.

Several evenings after our return to camp an old medicine man told me that, according to a vision he had had, he was collecting enough wolf skins for a big, wolf robe couch cover, and that I could go with him the next morning if I would like to see how he caught the animals. He had completed his trap the day before, and thought that there were already in it all the wolves that he needed.

Of course, I wanted to learn all I could about trapping, and so rode down the valley with him the next morning. About three miles below camp we entered a big, open bottom and he pointed to his trap, away out in the center of it. In the distance it appeared to be a round corral, and so it was, a corral of heavy eight-or nine-foot posts set closely together in the ground, and slanting inward at an angle of thirty or forty degrees. At the base the corral was about twelve feet in diameter. In one place a pile of rocks and earth was heaped against it, and when I saw that I did not need the old man's explanation of how he caught the wolves; they jumped into the corral from the earth slant to the top of it, enticed there by a pile of meat, and, once in, they could not jump high enough to get out.

Several wolves that were hanging about the corral ran away at our approach, and as we came close we could see that there were wolves in the corral. We dismounted, climbed the earth slope and looked in, and I could hardly believe my eyes when I saw that it held thirteen big wolves and a dead coyote. The latter had undoubtedly been the first to jump down for the bait, and the wolves had come later, and killed him. The wolves pretended to pay no attention to us, as we looked down upon them, milling around and sticking their noses into the interstices of the posts, but they had wary eyes upon us all the same. The old man got out his bow, and some all-wood arrows, the sharp tips fire hardened, and shot the wolves one by one without a miss, each shaft striking at one side of the backbone just back of the ribs and ranging down and forward into heart and lungs. Some of the animals struggled a bit, but all died without a whimper. When the last one fell he removed two posts that had simply been tied to those set firmly in the ground, and dragged the animals out through the opening one by one. I helped him skin them.

"There! I wanted eight, I have thirteen skins. My work is done; it is now for my woman to tan them and make the robe," he exclaimed.

"You will not replace the two posts, and put in fresh bait for more wolves?" I asked.

"No, I have all that I need," he answered. "Eight are enough for a big robe. I shall lie upon it, sleep upon it, and the strength that is in the wolves will become my strength, so my vision told me. I am well satisfied."

"And I am glad to have learned how to catch wolves," I told him, and we packed the skins upon our horses and went home. Years afterward, along in the 60's and 70's, when wolf skins went up to five dollars each, I somewhat improved upon the old man's corral trap, making mine of logs laid up to form a hollow pyramid about ten by sixteen feet at the base, and four by ten feet at the top. This was much more quickly and easily built than the stake corral, which involved the digging of a deep trench in which to set the stakes, and the building of an incline to the top. The wolves did not hesitate to step up from one to another of the inslanting logs and jump down upon the quantities of meat I placed inside, and there I had them. During one winter at St. Mary's Lakes, the winter of 1872-73, my sons and I caught more than seven hundred wolves in our pyramid log trap!

Although we saw nothing more of the Crows after their attack upon us, I kept thinking about them all the time. The big war party that had gone to raid their herds returned after a month or so without a single horse. They reported that the enemy was encamped some distance up the Bighorn River, and that their horses were under so heavy a guard both night and day that they had not dared attempt to stampede them. Before real winter set in another party of our warriors went out, and had no better success. The Crows were still close herding their horses in the daytime, and keeping them in well guarded corrals at night.

It was in our lone camp on Arrow River that this thought came to me: If the Blackfeet would only make peace with the Crows, the latter might then accompany us north and trade at our post. I asked myself if it was in any way possible for me to accomplish this. Well I knew what a grand coup it would be for me if I could ride into the post and say to the factor: "Here I am, returned with a good knowledge of the Blackfoot language. I have been far, and seen much. I have had the Pi-kun-i and the Crows, after a desperate fight, make peace with one another, and have induced that far tribe to come and trade with us. They are here!"

Well, when I thought that, I became so excited that it was long before I could sleep. I thought about it all the next day, and determined to speak to Red Crow about it. When evening came, and we had eaten our fill of is-sap-wot-sists, and were resting on our soft couches, I said to him: "Brother, how is peace made with an enemy tribe? Tell me all about it!"

"Ai! You shall know," he answered. "If there is much talk of peace, the chiefs get together and council about it, and if they decide that it will be good to make peace with the enemy, they send messengers with presents of pipes and tobacco to the enemy chiefs, asking that they smoke the pipe. If the enemy chiefs accept the pipe, and smoke the tobacco with it, then their answer is that they will be glad to make peace, and they tell the messengers where they and their people will meet our chiefs and our people, and make the peace."

"If your father and the other chiefs will make peace with the Crows, will you go with me to their camp?" I asked.

"I don't know that I want peace with them! It is good to have enemies to fight and count coup upon; that is what makes us men, brave warriors!" he exclaimed.

"Yes! And oh, how many poor and unhappy widows and fatherless children!" Mink Woman put in, much to my surprise.

"Brother, you shall know my heart!" I went on. "I want this peace to be made for two reasons. First, for the sake of the women and children, and all the old, dependent upon the hunters for their food and shelter. Second, I want the Crows to go north with us and trade at our post. I want all this very much. Now, say that you will help me; that you will do all that you can toward making the peace!"

"Oh, Brother! As you love me, say yes!" Mink Woman cried.

"We all want peace, we women! Peace with all tribes!" said Rattle Woman.

"Well, I say yes. I will do what I can. Not that I want peace, but because you ask me to help you!" he answered.

So it was that, upon our return to camp, we began to urge Lone Walker to make peace with the Crows. At first he just laughed at us. Then got cross whenever we mentioned the subject, and went off visiting to be rid of us. But we kept at him, with a larger and larger following of women, and even men, and at last he called the council, and after long argument the chiefs decided to send peace messengers to the Crow camp as soon as the first geese arrived in the spring. Mad Plume was to be the lead messenger, because it was his sister who had married into the Crow tribe. Another was Ancient Otter (Mis-sum-am-un-is) and Red Crow and I the other two. Lone Walker at first declared that we should not go; that the mission was too dangerous for boys to undertake; far more dangerous than going on a raid. But in that, too, we had our way. On a sunny, although cold day in March, a flock of geese was seen flying north over the camp, and the next day we started, well mounted, with an extra robe each, and the peace pipe and tobacco in a roll upon Mad Plume's back, beside his bow and arrow case.

Yes! You shall know all: As we rode out of camp, and I looked back at my comfortable lodge home, my heart went way, way down! On the previous evening I had been told the tale of some peace messengers to the Snakes some years before. Upon entering the enemy camp and stating their mission, they had been set upon and all killed but one, he being told to go straight home and tell the Pi-kun-i chiefs that that was the Snakes' answer to their offer. That might be, I thought, the kind of answer that the Crows would give us!

CHAPTER IX
THE COMING OF COLD MAKER

I well remember how warm and windless that March day was. There were patches of snow on the north side of the hills, and in the coulees, but otherwise the brown plains were bare and dry. The mountains, of course, were impassable, so we kept along the foot of them, traveling east, and that night camped at the foot of the Black Butte. The following morning we swung around the butte and headed south by a little east, a course that would take us to the junction of Elk River and the Bighorn, my companions said. We crossed the Musselshell River at noon or a little earlier, and that night slept upon the open plain. The weather continued fine. The next morning also broke clear and warm and cloudless. We started on at sunrise and, topping a ridge, Mad Plume pointed to some dark breaks away off to the south, and told me that they marked the course of Elk River. I estimated that we were about twenty miles from them.

At about ten o'clock we marked a big wedge of gray geese coming north, and Red Crow, pointing to them, exclaimed: "See the sun's messengers! He sends them north to tell us that he is coming to drive Cold Maker back to his always-winter land!"

He had no more than said that than the geese suddenly broke their well-ordered wedge lines and, shrilly honking, turned and went straight south on wild, uneven wings!

"Ha! They have seen Cold Maker coming! Yes! He is coming; I can smell him!" Mad Plume exclaimed, and brought his horse to a stand and looked to the north.

So did we, and saw a black belt of fog all across the horizon and right down upon the ground, and coming south with frightful speed. It had advanced as far as the north slope of the Snowy Mountains when we turned and saw it, and even as we looked they were lost in its blackness! The air suddenly became strong with the odor of burning grass. I had never seen anything like it. The swiftly moving, black fog bank, apparently turning over and over like a huge roller and blotting out the plain and mountains, frightened me, and I asked my companions what it meant.

"Fearful wind, cold, and snow! Cold Maker is bringing it! He hides himself in his black breath!" Red Crow told me.

"We have to ride hard! Unless we can get to the timber we are gone!" Mad Plume cried, and away we went as though we were trying to outride a big war party. And then suddenly that black fog bank struck us and instead of fog it was a terrific storm cloud! The wind all but tore us from our horses; fine, hard snow swirled and beat into our eyes, almost blinding us, and the air became bitterly cold. I marveled at the sudden change from sunny spring to a winter blizzard. Like my companions, I had on a pair of soft leather moccasins, and over them a pair of buffalo robe moccasins, and on my hands were robe mittens, but for all their thickness and warmth both hands and feet began to numb in the terrible cold of the storm.

Mad Plume led us, we following close in single file. In front of me, not ten feet away, Red Crow and his horse were but dim shadows in the driving snow. I saw him dismount and begin running beside his horse, and I got down and did likewise. And so, alternately on foot and riding we went on and on until it seemed to me that we had traveled thrice the distance to the river breaks that we had seen so plainly before the storm came up. At last Mad Plume stopped and we crowded around him. He had to shout to make himself heard. "What think you?" he asked. "Is the wind still from the north?"

We could not answer that. To me it seemed to be coming from all directions at once.

"If Cold Maker has changed it we are sure to become lost and die. If he still blows it south we should soon get to shelter," he said, and led on.

"We are lost!" I kept saying to myself as we ran, and rode, on and on for what seemed to me hours and hours, the snow at last becoming so deep that we were obliged to remain on our horses. But just as I felt that I was beginning to freeze, that there was no longer any use in trying to keep going, we began to descend a steep slope, and at the foot of it rode into a grove of big cottonwoods and out of the terrible wind! Mad Plume led us into a deep part of the woods where grew great clumps of tall willows, and we dismounted. "Ha! We survive! And now for comfort: a lodge, fire, food! Hobble your horses and get to work!" he cried.

I couldn't hobble mine, my hands were so numb that I could do nothing with them; so I ran around swinging them and clapping them together until they became warm. I then cared for my horse, and with good will helped my companions gather material, dry poles, dead branches, brush, and armfuls of tall rye grass for a small lodge. We soon had it up and a good fire going. The cold air rushed in through a thousand little spaces between the poles; we made a lodge lining of our pishimores—pieces of buffalo robe that we used for saddle blankets—and sat back on our rye grass couches and were truly comfortable, and very thankful that Cold Maker had not overcome us! Presently one of our horses nickered, and Red Crow went out to learn the cause of it. "A big herd of elk has come in!" he called to us, and we all ran out and followed him on their trail; they had passed within fifty yards of the lodge. We soon saw them standing in a thick patch of willows, heads down, and bodies all humped up with the cold. They paid no attention to our approach and we moved right up close to them and shot down four with bows and arrows. We skinned them all, taking the hides for more lodge covering, and cut a lot of meat from a fat, dry cow that I had killed, and then we were prepared to weather the storm, no matter how long it should last.

The terrible wind and snow lasted all that night and far into the afternoon of the following day, and when it ceased the weather remained piercingly cold. When the sun came out I took up my gun and went for a walk, and going through the timber looked out upon a great river, the Sieur de la Vérendrie's *La Roche Jaune*, (the Yellowstone). He had seen it, where it merged with the Missouri, in 1744, and upon his return to Montreal told of the mighty flow of its waters from the snows of the Shining Mountains. How many times I had heard my grandfather and others speak of it, and even talk of an expedition to explore its vast solitudes to its source. They were sure that they would be well rewarded with furs. The very name of the river suggested riches; rich mines of gold and silver! And here I was, actually upon the shore of this great river of the West, looking out upon its frozen stretches, and in quest of neither furs nor gold, but of peace between two warring tribes! I said to myself that the Sieur de la Vérendrie and his men, and Lewis and Clark and their men had seen the mouth of the river, but that mine was the honor of first seeing its upper reaches, and oh, how proud of that I was! I did not learn until long afterward that upon their return journey from the Western Ocean, a part of the Lewis and Clark expedition had struck across the plains to the river, and followed it down to the Missouri.

I returned to the lodge to find my companions roasting our evening meal of elk ribs, and was soon eating my large share of the fat meat. When that was over we made plans for continuing our journey. While I had been out at the river, Mad Plume had climbed to the rim of the plain for a look at the country, and found that we were not far above the mouth of the Bighorn.

Said Mad Plume now: "No matter how cold it is in the morning, we must start on. The colder it is the safer we will be, for we will not likely be discovered by the Crow hunters, and that is what I most fear, discovery of us while traveling, and sudden attack upon us. I think that if we can reach the edge of the camp without being seen, we can go on through it to the chief's lodge safely enough; the people will be so curious to know why we have come that they will not then fall upon us."

"We can travel nights and escape being seen," said Ancient Otter.

"But we can't cover up our tracks; this fall of snow will last for some days. Well, we will make an early start, and anyhow keep traveling in the daytime if we find it possible," Mad Plume decided, and started to talk about other matters.

After a time Ancient Otter said: "Our camping here reminds me of the time that we made peace with the Crows just below, at the mouth of the Bighorn, and the young Crow, Little Wolf, with whom I became very friendly. I wonder if he is still living? I did not see him when we had that fight, some moons back. If he is still alive I know that he will be with us for making peace. I must tell you about him:

"On the evening of the day that we made peace, he invited me to dance with him and his friends, and I had a pleasant time. A day or two after that I asked him to one of our dances. Then we visited often in his lodge and in mine, and we became close friends. One day he said to me, in signs, of course, the Crows are fine sign talkers, 'We are five young men going south on a raid; you get together four of your friends and join us.'

"Two or three days after that we started, five Crows and five of us, Little Wolf and I joint leaders of the party. We went on foot, traveling at night, taking our time; we had the whole summer before us. We followed up the Bighorn almost to its head, then crossed a wide, high ridge and struck a stream heading in several mountain canyons, and running east into the great plain. At the mouth of one of the canyons we discovered a big camp of the enemy. We came upon it unexpectedly, soon after daylight, and after crossing a wide, level stretch of plain. Looking down from the edge of the cliff we had come to, there was the camp right under us. People were already up and moving about, some of the men preparing to ride out to hunt. We dared not attempt to go back across the plain; there was but one thing for us to do; we wriggled down into a patch of cherry brush just below the top of the cliff and in a coulee that broke it, and felt safe enough except for the fact that the brush was heavy with ripe fruit; some women and children might come up to gather it.

"The cliff was broken down in many places, more a steep slope of boulders than a cliff, and it was not high. From where we sat in the brush the nearest lodges of the camp were no more than long bow shot from us. We could see the people plainly and hear them talking. They were the Spotted Horses People.[1]

[1]Kish-tsi-pim-i-tup-i. Spotted Horses People. The Cheyennes.

"The lodge nearest us was very large, new, and evidently the lodge of a medicine man, for it was painted with figures of two long snakes with plumes on their heads. A number of women lived in it; they kept coming out and going back, but their man never once appeared.

"The horses of the camp were grazing in the valley of the stream both above and below it and we looked at them with longing, for we could see that many of them were of the spotted breed. After a time a boy on a big, dancing, spotted stallion drove a large band of horses up in front of the snake medicine lodge and then the medicine man came out to look at them. He was a very tall and heavily built man. He wore a cow leather wrap, medicine painted. My Crow friend nudged me, pointed to the big stallion and then signed to me: 'I shall take that horse to-night, and others with him!'

"I laughed, and signed back, 'You don't know that for sure. I may be the one to seize him!'

"The medicine man was talking to the boy on the stallion, louder and louder until his voice became like the roar of a wounded bear in our ears. He suddenly reached up and seized the boy by the arm, dragged him from the stallion, and then picking up a big stick began to beat him with it. We groaned at the awful sight; almost we cried out at it, we who never strike our sons. The women had come out of the lodge; they were crying, no doubt begging the man to let the boy go, but he paid no attention to them, nor to the crowd of people hurrying toward him from all parts of the camp. He beat and beat the boy, at last struck him on the head and he fell as though dead; and at that the women ran forward and lifted him and hurried him into a near-by lodge. The man watched them go, then took up his fallen wrap and went into his lodge. Said my Crow friend to me, in signs, 'We must make that man pay big for beating the boy. He shall lose his horses, all of them, and his medicine, too!'

"'Yes! Let us, you and I, take all his horses, and our men take others as they will. But his medicine, no, not that; it would bring us bad luck,' I answered.

"All that long, hot day, thirsty, hungry, we sat there in the patch of cliff brush watching the enemy camp and its horse herds. We saw nothing more of the beaten boy, and the medicine man did not appear again until nearly sunset. He then went down the valley to his herd, which had been allowed to graze back to its feeding ground, and caught out of it the stallion, rode it home and picketed it close to his lodge. Other men brought in one or two of their horses for early morning use. The sun set. The moon came up. We climbed back to the top of the cliff, went along it for some distance, and then down into the valley below the camp to water. There, where we struck the river, was to be our meeting place. After a long wait we scattered out, Little Wolf and I going together after the medicine man's herd. We had kept constant watch on it, and now went straight to it and drove it to the meeting place. Some of our companions were already there with their takings. We left the herd for them to hold, and struck out for the camp to get the big stallion. On the way up my friend again told me that he would take the medicine. I tried to get him to leave it alone, but his mind was set; the loss of the medicine, he said, should be the man's punishment for beating the boy.

"The lodge fires had all died out and the people were asleep when we arrived at the edge of the camp. We kept close to the foot of the cliff and approached the medicine man's lodge. The stallion was picketed between it and the cliff. Little Wolf signed to me to go to it and wait for him while he took the medicine, which we could see was still hanging on a tripod just back of the lodge. Again I signed him not to take it. I laid hold of his arm and tried to lead him with me toward the horse, but he signed that he *would* have the medicine and I let him go, and went on toward the horse.

"I don't know why I changed my course and followed my friend; something urged me to do so. I was about twenty steps behind him as he went up to the tripod and started to lift the medicine sacks from it. As he did so I saw the lodge skin suddenly raised and the medicine man sprang out from under it and seized him from behind. I ran to them as they struggled and struck the big man on the head with my gun and down he went and lay still. He had never seen me, and never knew what hit him. Neither had he made any outcry. As soon as he fell we ran to the stallion, bridled him with his picket rope and sprang upon his back, Little Wolf behind me, and still hanging to the medicine sacks. It was my intention to make the stallion carry us out from the camp as fast as he could go, but there was nowhere any outcry—any one in sight, so I let him go at a walk until we were some distance down the valley, and then hurried him the rest of the way to the meeting place. Our companions were all there with their takings, mounted and waiting for us. Little Wolf got down and caught a horse and away we went for the north, and it was a big band of horses that we drove ahead of us.

"At daybreak we stopped to change to fresh horses, and as I turned loose the stallion I signed to Little Wolf: 'There! Take your horse!'

"'I shall never put a rope on him! You saved my life; that enemy would have killed me but for you. The horse is yours,' he signed back, and went away off our trail and hung the medicine sacks in the brush where any pursuers we might have would never see them. He gave them to the sun.

"Well, when we got back to the mouth of the Bighorn we found that the Pi-kun-i had started for the Snow Mountains several days before, so after one night in the Crow camp we five took up their trail. I spent that last night in Little Wolf's lodge, and we planned to meet often again, and to go on more raids together. His last words, or signs, rather, to me were: 'Do not forget that no matter what others may do, you and I shall always be friends!'

"'Yes! Friends always,' I answered, and rode away. I have never seen him since that time."

So ended Ancient Otter's story. It heartened me. If his friend was still alive—and he certainly had not been killed in the big fight—he would be with us for making peace, as well as Mad Plume's sister. Said Mad Plume to me: "You now know why Ancient Otter is with us. He told the story to you; we knew it!"

The next morning broke very cold; the air was full of fine frost flakes; the snow was drifted and in places very deep. We unhobbled our horses, saddled them and struck off through the timber toward the mouth of the Bighorn soon after sunrise. An hour or so later we crossed the river on the ice, and turned up the valley of the Bighorn. Here I again said to myself that I was traversing country that people of my race had never seen, but I was mistaken. I learned years afterward that a Lewis and Clark man, named Cotter, had come west again in 1807, and had trapped on the headwaters of the Bighorn, and followed it down to its junction with the Yellowstone.

We saw great numbers of the different kinds of game that morning, and the sight that most impressed me was the trees full of grouse, or prairie chickens, as the whites call them. We passed hundreds of cottonwoods in which the birds were almost as plentiful as apples in an apple tree. They sat motionless upon their perches, their feathers all fluffed out, and paid not the slightest attention to us as we passed under them.

"They are cold and unhappy now, but in the next moon they will be dancing, and happy enough," Red Crow said to me. He saw that I thought he was joking, and went on: "Yes, dancing! They gather in a circle on the plain and the males dance and the females look on. Oh, they have just as good times dancing as we do."

He was right. Many a time since then I have stopped and watched the birds dance for a long time. It is a very interesting sight. After the long years I have passed in the plains and mountains, studying the habits of all wild creatures, I become impatient when I hear people speak of them as dumb creatures. Dumb! Why, they have their racial languages as well as we! If they hadn't, do you think, for instance, that the grouse could have learned their peculiar dance? Or the beavers how to build their wonderful dams and houses?

The snow was so deep that we made no more than fifteen miles that day. We hobbled the tired horses long before sunset, and put up another war lodge and made ourselves as comfortable as was possible. We had seen no signs of the Crows during the day.

It was the next afternoon that we sighted them, or rather, one rider turning down into the valley from the plain, and several miles ahead of us. We happened at the time to be in the upper end of a long grove, and, while we could see him plainly, we were sure that the trees screened us from him, bare though they were.

"The sun is almost down, he rides as if he were in no hurry; I think that the camp cannot be far away," said Ancient Otter.

"Ai! That is my thought," Mad Plume agreed, and led on, the rider having passed from our sight around a bend in the valley. We crossed a strip of open bottom, entered another grove which circled clear around the bend, and presently, looking out from the upper end of it, saw the great camp. It was pitched in a wide, open bottom about a mile from us and was in two sections, or circles, one, of course, that of the River Crows, the other the Mountain Crows. Looking out upon them, and the swarms of people passing in all directions among the lodges, I shivered a bit. Not until that moment had I been even doubtful of the success of our mission. Now a great fear came over me. Many of those people I saw were mourning for the loss of some dear one in the attack upon us some months back. I doubted that they would ever give us time to state the reason of our coming; they would kill us as soon as they saw that we were the hated Pi-kun-i! And then, to add to my fear, Mad Plume turned to Ancient Otter and asked: "Brother, which one, think you, is the camp of the Mountain Crows?"

"I can't make out for sure, but I think it is the first one. We have to make sure of that. If we enter the camp of the River Crows we shall find no one there to help us; right there will be our end!"

"Your sister and Little Wolf are in the Mountain Crow camp?" I asked Mad Plume.

"Yes!" he answered, very shortly, and continued staring thoughtfully at the camps.

Said Ancient Otter: "Oh, if we could only be a little nearer to the lodges, I could tell. Little Wolf's lodge is on the west side of the camp circle, and right next it, the first one to the south, is a lodge painted with two wolves. The Crow wolf medicine."

"Yes, I remember that lodge. It is five lodges north of my sister's lodge," said Mad Plume.

"Well, one thing we can do! Unless we freeze to death!" Mad Plume went on. "We can stay right here until night, then sneak into camp and find my sister and your friend and get them to help us, to protect us until we are in the chief's lodge."

We all agreed that that was the only thing to do, and began our chilly wait. Red Crow pointed to the many bands of horses grazing between the camp and us, and on both slopes of the valley. "What a chance for us if we were raiders!" he exclaimed.

"Don't talk foolishness at this time!" Mad Plume told him. "It is best that you pray the gods for help in what we are about to undertake!" And with that he voiced a short, earnest prayer to the sun, to Old Man, and his own medicine animal—"thou little under water animal"—he called it, to preserve us from all the dangers that we were to face there in the enemy camp. And when he had finished I cried out even as the others did: "Ai! Spuhts-uh Mut-tup-i, kim-o-ket-an-nan!" (Yes! Above People, pity have for us!)

Hai! Hai! But it was cold! Our horses stood humped up and miserable, the sweat freezing on their hair.

"We have to hobble them and turn them loose to graze, else they will freeze to death," said Mad Plume.

"Yes, we may as well do that. If all goes well with us we shall find them safe enough hereabout, and if we never come back for them, why, they will live anyhow!" said Ancient Otter. So we turned them out, and set our saddles and ropes and pishimores in a little pile, and stamped about and swung our arms trying to keep warm.

Oh, how slowly, and yet how fast the sun went down that evening. But down it went at last, and as soon as the valley was really dark we started for the camp. As we neared it Mad Plume's last words were: "Remember this: You are to expect abuse and you are to stand it until you see that there is no hope for us. Then, *die fighting*!"

Cheering words, weren't they!

CHAPTER   X
MAKING PEACE WITH THE CROWS

We approached the lower camp, the lodges all yellow glow from the cheerful fires within. And a cheerful camp it was; men and women singing here and there, several dances going on, children laughing and playing—and some squalling—men shouting out to their friends to come and smoke with them. We could see many dim figures hurrying through the cold and darkness from one lodge to another. We approached the west side of the circle at a swift walk, just as though we belonged there—knew where we were going; in that piercing cold to loiter, to hesitate, would be to proclaim that we were strangers in the camp. The circle was fifteen or twenty well separated lodges in width, so we had to go far into it in order to see the inside lodges. Ancient Otter led us, looking for the lodge of the painted wolves. We were well into the circle when a man came out of a lodge that we were just passing, and my heart gave a big jump when the door curtain was thrust aside and he stepped out. He saw us, of course, but turned and went off the way we had come, and I breathed more freely. But we had not gone two lodges farther when we saw some one coming straight toward us. We had to keep on. We drew our robes yet more closely about our faces. It was an anxious moment. We were due to meet the person right in front of a well-lighted lodge, and were within a few steps of it when a number of men inside struck up a song. When opposite our leader the person said something, and half stopped; but Ancient Otter pretended that he did not hear and kept right on, we following. Then, just as I was passing the person, he did stop and stare at us! I dared not look back, and oh, how I wanted to! I expected every step I made to hear a shout of alarm that would arouse the camp. But no! We went peacefully on, and presently Ancient Otter led us out of the circle, and away out from the lodges, and when at a safe distance stopped and told us that we had been in the wrong camp; the camp of the River Crows.

"Never mind! We have had two escapes! The gods are with us! Lead on!" Mad Plume told him.

"Yes, I go! Follow, brothers, and pray! Pray for help!" he exclaimed.

We made a wide circle around to the other camp to avoid any persons who might be going from one to the other of the two, and presently struck it on the west side of the circle. No one was in sight so we went straight in among the lodges and soon saw the one of the wolf medicine, the light of the fire within revealing plainly the big wolf painting on the right of the doorway. It had the appearance of great ferocity, the wide mouth showing long, sharp fangs. Ancient Otter stopped and pointed to the lodge and said to us in a low tone: "There it is, the wolf medicine lodge, and that one just to the north of it is my friend's lodge. Come! We will go in!"

"No! It is best that we go to my sister's lodge first. We will need some one to interpret for us at once, and I am sure that by this time she speaks Crow," said Mad Plume.

Now, this should all have been arranged beforehand, for while we stood there talking a man suddenly came around a lodge behind us and called out to us something or other in his language. We pretended not to hear him.

"You haven't time to get to your sister's lodge! Follow me!" said Ancient Otter, and we started on at a swift walk. But the Crow came faster; something in our appearance, and our silence when he addressed us had aroused his suspicions. As Ancient Otter raised the door curtain of the lodge and the light streamed out full in his face, the man recognized him as one of the hated Pi-kun-i and shouted—as I afterwards learned—that the enemy were in the camp, and as we hurried into the lodge we heard on all sides of it the answering, rallying cry of the warriors.

When Ancient Otter stepped into the lodge and the Crow, Little Wolf, saw who it was, he sprang up and embraced and kissed him, then did the same to us and motioned us to seats. We took them, but it was hard to do so with the rallying cries of the warriors and screams of frightened women and children ringing in our ears. As soon as we were seated Little Wolf signed his friend: "You have come! I am glad!"

"I am glad to see you! We are sent by our chiefs to propose peace to your chiefs. Help us! First, send for the woman of the Pi-kun-i, sister of the chief there, Mad Plume."

"Yes!" Little Wolf signed, and spoke to one of his women, and she hurried out. He spoke to another, and as she went out he signed to us, "I am sending that one for our chiefs! Now, sit you here! I go to stand outside and keep the crazy warriors back." And with that he snatched up his bow case, drew out the bow and a handful of arrows, and ran outside, thrusting back a man entering as he reached the doorway. He went none too soon; a great crowd was gathering about the lodge, shouting angrily, crying for our scalps, no doubt. We held our weapons ready and kept our eyes on the lodge skin, expecting every moment that the warriors would raise it and pour in upon us. I tell you, that was an anxious time. I must have shown that I was terribly frightened, for Mad Plume gave my shoulder a pat and said to me: "Take courage, younger brother, take courage!"

Just then the door curtain was thrust aside and a handsome young woman rushed in, and Mad Plume sprang up and embraced her. She clung to him, crying: "Oh, my brother! What a risk for you to come here at this time! Oh, I hope that all will be well with us! My man is out there with Little Wolf, holding back the warriors! Oh, why don't the chiefs come! Oh, they have come! Listen!"

The noise outside had suddenly died down; some one was addressing the crowd in a deep and powerful voice, and in a minute or two she said to us: "It is the head chief, Spotted Bull. He commands his head warriors to see that you are not harmed, and tells the others to all go home!"

And then, a little later: "They are going; they are minding him! Oh, I am glad! For the present you are safe!"

Again, the door curtain was raised and Little Wolf came in, followed by a young man who hurried to greet Mad Plume. Red Crow told me that it was his brother-in-law. In turn he gave us greeting. Then Little Wolf's wives returned, and he ordered them to hurry and set food before us, which they presently did, big wooden bowls full of boiled boss ribs of buffalo. I should have been hungry; perhaps I was, but I was so excited and anxious that I ate only a few mouthfuls. Presently we heard some one talking loudly outside the doorway. Little Wolf answered him, and then spoke to Mad Plume's sister, telling her to interpret, and she said to us: "Spotted Bull sends you word that the chiefs will council together to-morrow morning, and then have a talk with you."

"Yes. I told Spotted Bull that you were peace messengers from your chiefs," Little Wolf signed to us.

After the meal was over there was some talk, Mad Plume's sister interpreting, and then it was decided that Ancient Otter should sleep in his friend's lodge, and that we three should be the guests of Mad Plume's brother-in-law. Accordingly we went over to his lodge, big, and well fitted out with soft, robe couches, and Mad Plume and his sister fell to talking. She first had to hear all about her relatives and friends, who had died, and how the living were doing. She then told about the Crows, and her life with them. She said that her man was very kind to her, that she was perfectly happy except for the fact that, owing to the continuous war between the Crows and the Pi-kun-i, she could not occasionally visit her relatives. As to the last fight, she said that a big war party had started out on the trail of some Snakes, who had taken a large herd of horses, and while after them had discovered the Pi-kun-i moving out from Arrow River without the usual line of warriors in the lead of the column, and so had made the attack. And at that her man, who was listening, understanding considerable of her language, told her to tell us that the people who had lost relatives in the fight were still mourning, and he feared that they might win over the chiefs to refuse our peace pipe. She added that she thought most of the women would want peace, and that she would go among them early in the morning, and get them to urge their men to talk for it.

That was about all Red Crow and I heard of the talk. Tired out, and made drowsy by the comfortable heat of the lodge, a great change from the bitter cold that we had experienced, we fell asleep. And we slept soundly under the assurance that the Crow chief's guards were in the lodges on either side of us.

Early the next morning, right after preparing food for us, Mad Plume's sister went out on her round of talks for peace, and soon afterward some of the Crow men began to drop in for a chat and smoke, and especially ask about certain of the Pi-kun-i with whom they had become very friendly in time of peace. I was surprised and pleased at the large number of these visitors; it was proof that there were many in the camp who would be on the side of peace. Another thing that surprised me was the elegance of dress of these men. Without exception they wore beautiful quill-embroidered shirts and leggings and moccasins, garments that our people put on only on great occasions. And if anything they were even taller, more graceful, and with more pride in their bearing than the men of the Blackfeet tribes, and that is saying much. They were all apparently much interested in me, wanting to know all that my friends could tell them about my presence in the country, and why one so young should be a peace messenger. To that last question Mad Plume answered that, when the time for it came, I would probably tell my reason for being there. After a time Ancient Otter came in with his friend, Little Wolf, and we anxiously awaited the call from the council of chiefs.

When noon came, and there was still no word from them, our anxiety increased. Then Mad Plume's sister returned and told us to take courage. Both Spotted Bull and Lone Runner, chief of the River Crows, and some of the clan chiefs of both tribes, were for accepting the peace pipe, but that other clan chiefs, and a good number of warriors wanted the pipe sent back. The objectors to peace were mostly those who had lost relatives in the Arrow River fight. She thought that these would eventually do as the head chiefs desired.

It was not until late afternoon that a messenger called us to the council. We went over to the big lodge accompanied by Little Wolf, and Mad Plume's brother-in-law and sister, the latter to act as interpreter. There was an immense crowd in the camp, most of the River Crows having come up to hear all about the peace talk, and many that we passed stared at us with anything but friendly eyes. Had it not been for our guard of warriors coming right behind us, we might never have reached the council lodge.

We were not greeted with smiles or any word of welcome when we entered the lodge and took the seats left vacant for us, but, not at all daunted, Mad Plume leaned forward and placed the peace pipe and tobacco in front of Spotted Bull, and said: "Lone Walker, your friend, sends you this pipe and tobacco, with these words: 'Peace is good, and war is bad! Let us smoke together and each declare that there shall be peace between the Crow Tribes and the Blackfeet Tribes.'"

"Ai! Learning from our young man, Little Wolf, that you had come with an offer of peace from our good friend, Lone Walker, we have been considering the matter all day," Spotted Bull answered. "From the beginning my brother there, chief of our brother tribe, and I have talked for peace, and so have many of our clan chiefs. But a few still hold out that between us and the Blackfeet tribes there can be no peace."

"You mean me when you say that!" exclaimed one of the clan chiefs, a big, haughty appearing, flashing eyed man. "Yes! I hold out for war, war always between us and the Pi-kun-i! And I am not alone in that desire; I can go out in this camp and bring you many, very many men who think as I do!"

Now, when Mad Plume's sister had told us what this man said, Mad Plume then, much to my surprise, told her to say to the chief that he would like to have his friend, Rising Wolf, the white youth, speak a few words to the council. She did so, and Spotted Bull replied, "Yes! Let us hear what he has to say!"

I considered a moment or two. My first thought was to tell the council that they were not powerful enough to fight the Blackfeet tribes, and their Gros Ventre and Sak-si allies. But I said to myself that that wouldn't do. Nothing had even been said of the flight of the Crows, their abandonment of much of their property after the Arrow River fight. At last I said to the interpreter, "Tell them this for me:

"I would like to see peace made on account of the women and children! In war they suffer, not you men. I have been sick ever since that Arrow River fight, for I then saw women and girls and even children killed as well as men! White men do not do that! They would sooner die than kill women! They believe that it is only cowards who kill women.

"This is a great country. There is plenty of room in it for the Crow tribes and the Blackfeet tribes, and game enough upon the plains and in the mountains for all. Then why fight? Why keep the women and children mourning for loss of father and brother and son? Now, my Red Coat chief wants the Crows and the Blackfeet and all different tribes to be friends with one another, and friendly with him. From the Far East he has come with guns, and tobacco, and all kinds of goods, and built a white man's lodge on Bow River, and he wants you all to come there and smoke and feast with him, and give him your beaver skins for his guns and other things. You Crows can't do that if you are at war with the Blackfeet. I say this: Make peace, and be happy."

While the woman was interpreting that I asked Mad Plume if it would not be well for him to offer to give back to the Crows the lodges and things that we had taken after their flight.

"No. About everything has been used up, and they have new lodges. And I don't think that they want to be reminded that they fled from us," he answered.

Just then the woman finished speaking and I happened to be looking across at the man who had declared that he was for war, always war! A great change had taken place in him as he listened. Instead of hatred and defiance, his eyes now expressed great interest, intense desire; and leaning forward he said to Spotted Bull, as I afterward learned, "Lift the pipe! Fill, and light it!"

Spotted Bull looked around at the circle and asked: "Is that what you all say?"

"Yes! Yes!" they answered, and he took the pipe from its wrappings, cut some of the tobacco, mixed it with dried red willow bark, filled the bowl, and after lighting the pipe and taking a few whiffs, passed it to Mad Plume, saying: "Let us smoke together. Tell my good friend, Lone Walker, that there shall be peace between him and me, between his children and mine, and that as soon as it is warm enough for us to travel we will go and camp beside him and hold the peace council with him and his chiefs."

Mad Plume took a few whiffs of smoke, then started the pipe on the round of the circle, and answered: "I am glad to have that word to take back to him. All you chiefs here, remember this, when you come, my lodge is your lodge. We shall have many smokes together!"

Suitable replies were made to that. Then the fierce chief asked many questions about the Red Coats' trading post, and the price in beaver skins of different articles. And then, a little later, the council broke up and we returned to Little Wolf's lodge, much pleased at the success of our mission.

Said Mad Plume's sister, "It was your talk that won them over, Rising Wolf."

"I am glad of that! I hoped that my talk about the poor women would do some good," I answered.

She laughed. "It was your talk about guns that they heard, not what you said about the women! More than anything else the Crows want guns," she said.

That very evening a Chinook wind set in, so we decided to make an early start for home. We wanted to get across Elk River, the Yellowstone, before the ice went out. Mad Plume's sister was so anxious to see her people again that she prevailed upon her man to take her with us, lodge and all; and Ancient Otter's friend, Little Wolf, came with us with his lodge and outfit, so we were quite a party. The two Crow tribes were to break camp three days later, and follow us. If there were any men still angry that the chiefs had accepted the peace pipe, we felt safe enough from them now that we had two lodges of their people with us, and accordingly we set out in high spirits, and, traveling leisurely, arrived in our own camp five days later. We were received with great acclaim, and as soon as it was learned that our mission was successful, that the Crows would soon be with us, great preparations for their reception went forward. Dearly they loved these opportunities for the spectacular, the dramatic incidents of life, and made the most of them.

When the Crows came, they halted some miles out from the river and put on all their finery, the men their war costumes, the women their beautiful, quill-embroidered, elk-tush-decorated gowns. Our scouts reported that they were coming, so we all dressed in our best and mounting our most lively horses went out to meet them. Lone Walker and his Bull band of the All Friends Society led, of course, all the other bands following. The women remained in camp, all but Mad Plume's sister, who rode in the rear of the Bull band, ready to act as interpreter.

We topped the slope up to the plain and found the great column of riders right close to us. They struck up a mighty song, a Crow song of greeting and peace, suddenly halted it, and then we sang the Blackfeet song of peace. And so, alternately singing, we approached one another, and at last met and the chiefs of both sides sprang from their horses and embraced one another. Then said Lone Walker, the woman interpreting, "My brothers! Because you and your children have come, this is a happy day for me and my children. We make you welcome. Come. Let us ride in to my lodge and smoke the pipe of peace together!"

Replying for both Crow tribes, Spotted Bull then answered: "Your words are straight. This is a happy day. We are glad to be with you, we shall be glad to smoke the peace pipe with you."

"Then let us mount and ride in. My lodge is your lodge. The pipe awaits you there," said Lone Walker, and they all mounted and led off, and we, holding back, fell in here and there with the long column of warriors and escorted them to our camp. In every lodge a feast and smokes awaited them, and while the chiefs counciled together, and smoked the peace pipe, and feasted, they were well entertained. And meantime, out in the big flat of Warm Spring Creek, their women were putting up their camp. The lodges were soon set, and then, even as the men were doing, the women of both camps renewed friendships, and exchanged presents and gossip. They were all expert sign talkers, as well as their men. It was, indeed, a happy time. A number of dances were held that afternoon, and I joined in the one that my band gave, and some of Lone Walker's women told me that I was a very graceful dancer. Well, I believe that I was.

On the following morning Lone Walker dispatched messengers to the chief of the Kai-na tribe, over on the Missouri, advising him of the peace that had been made with the Crows, and asking that he and some of his chiefs come over to meet the Crow chiefs, and to make plans for the return to the fort of the Red Coats. They came in due time, and more feasts and smokes, and more dances were held in their honor. At the council it was decided that the Kai-na, with the River Crows, should follow up the Missouri to the mountains, and trap northward along them, and that we, with the Mountain Crows, should go by the way of the gap between the Bear Paw and Wolf Mountains to Little River, and follow that up to the main range, and thence north to the post.

With the Mountain Crows, then, we crossed the Missouri at a place later named by the whites, Cow Island, the place where, in 1877, the Nez Percés made one of their last stands. From there we followed up the Stahk-tsi-kye-e-tuk-tai (River-in-the-Middle), which heads in the low gap dividing the Bear Paw and the Wolf Mountains, and thence went down to Little, or, as the whites say, Milk River. And here again I was in country that none of my race had ever seen.

Spring had now come. The days were warm and sunny, green grass was sprouting, buffaloes and antelopes covered the plains on all sides of us, the stream was alive with beavers, and so we were happy. The Crows had no traps, but nevertheless they kept gathering in nearly as many beaver pelts as we did with traps, simply by careful stalking, and long waiting, and good shooting with bow and arrows.

We were more than a month following up the river to its head. We then dropped over onto the St. Mary's Lakes (the Lakes Inside), trapped there for a time, and then went slowly northward, and ahead of the Kai-na and the River Crows. When the camp was still two days travel from the fort, Red Crow and I hurried on and, on the morning of the second day, suddenly appeared before Factor Hardesty as he sat in the sun just outside the gate of the fort.

"Bless me! It is little Hugh Monroe!" he cried, springing up and grasping my hand as I slid from my horse. "Well, well! Tell me quick! Did you get to the Missouri plains—and saw you any traders there?"

"I have been far beyond the Missouri! Away south of it to Elk River, the Sieur de la Vérendrie's *La Roche Jaune*, you know, and seen not one trader!" I answered. But I could not wait for him to ask questions. I poured out my tale of the vast country I had seen, its wealth of furs, our trouble with the Crows, and how we had made peace with them and they were coming to trade with us; and how he and the gathering of employees behind him did stare at me!

"When are they coming—the Crows and Pi-kun-i?" he asked.

"The River Crows and the Kai-na later on, the others, the Mountain Crows and the Pi-kun-i, to-day," I answered.

And at that he whirled upon the men and cried: "Hear ye that, now! Two tribes coming to-day. Go get your women busy cooking pots of meat for a feast to the chiefs. Put pipe and tobacco in my room! Run up the flag! Draw the shot from the cannon so that we can salute them and no one be hurt!"

The men flew to do his bidding, and then he had me for an hour or more telling him my adventures, and even then I had hardly begun.

"That will do for now! You have done well," he said at last, "so very well, my boy, that back you go with the Pi-kun-i for another winter in the South!"

And so ended my first year upon the plains.

THE END

Manufactured by Amazon.ca
Bolton, ON

31291374R00068